Teaching Music Musically

'Keith Swanwick is clear-headed in his analysis of the state of 'the art' of music education.'

'There are countless gems within these pages . . . has much of the essence of what music teachers need.'

Patricia Shehan Campbell, Professor of Music, University of Washington

This book is intended for music educators, including practising and intending teachers in schools and colleges and instrumental instructors.

The book is equally for anyone who invents or performs music, and for those who are curious about the ways in which we respond to music. It should find its way to those interested in the value and function of music, to professionals in the growing fields of music psychology and sociology. Ideas here will stimulate those who do not necessarily think of themselves as 'teachers' in a formal sense, but who are in some way involved in the world of music.

- The first two chapters are concerned with music itself, with its value and metaphorical significance and with the social context of musical understanding. These are important issues for musicians and music educators.
- The central chapters focus on music education. Through practical examples Keith Swanwick teases out the layers of musical experiences and sets out fundamental principles for music educators whatever the context of music teaching. In many countries demand for accountability has led to the development of state guidelines, national curricula or 'standards'. Valid and reliable assessment of students' work has become a vital issue. These implications are addressed in an imaginative and practical way.
- The book ends with a consideration of the relationship between institutionalised music education and the wider con   ch formal music education in schools and colle   d.

Keith Swanwick is Professor of Music Ed   n, Institute of Education.

D1421514

Teaching Music Musically

Keith Swanwick

London and New York

First published 1999
by Routledge
2 Park Square, Milton Park, Abingdon, Oxon, OX14 4RN

Simultaneously published in the USA and Canada
by Routledge
270 Madison Ave, New York NY 10016

Transferred to Digital Printing 2006

Typeset in Sabon by
M Rules

British Library Cataloguing in Publication Data
A catalogue record for this book is available from the British Library

Library of Congress Cataloging in Publication Data
Swanwick, Keith.
Teaching music musically/Keith Swanwick.
    p.   cm.
Includes bibliographical references and index.
1. Music – Instruction and study. 2. Title.
MT1.S946   1999
780'.71–dc21   98–33454 CIP MN

ISBN 0 415 19935 2 (hbk)
ISBN 0 415 19936 0 (pbk)

Printed and bound by CPI Antony Rowe, Eastbourne

Contents

Illustrations

Figures

Music examples

Acknowledgements

No book is an island. I am conscious of the many people who have influenced my thinking, sometimes by disagreeing and challenging and often by affirming and encouraging. Here I can name but a few of them.

First I wish to express my gratitude to Patricia Shehan Campbell and her colleagues. The position of Visiting Professor conferred by the University of Washington in the spring of 1998 was a lifeline. For several weeks I had the opportunity to read, write and teach in the most congenial surroundings, free from the constraints of normal routine. During this residency I was able to make real progress on the first draft of the book. The management of the Institute of Education in the University of London generously gave me study leave to complete the book. The Institute has facilitated my research and writing over a considerable period of time and I am very appreciative of this support.

I must acknowledge the contribution of many research students at the Institute of Education, London University, especially those who worked with me as their supervisor. It would be difficult to single out from many successful PhD students those whose research has made a particular contribution to my own work. However, I have to say that this book would not be as it is without the careful observations by June Boyce Tillman of children composing, or the further insights into children's musical development in the work of Michael Stavrides and Liane Hentschke. A recent study by Cecilia Cavalieri França on the relative contribution to musical understanding of performing, composing and audience-listening makes a very significant contribution to the fourth chapter. Also I must thank two of our research officers: Christine Jarvis who worked on the Tower Hamlets project – briefly described in the third chapter – and Dorothy Lawson who collected so much valuable data on the South Bank Centre project, without which the final chapter would be the poorer.

I am deeply indebted to numerous musicians, teachers, academics and students on various courses for their part in stimulating, challenging, disturbing and reassuring over several decades. I hope they will recognise in these pages something of their own intellectual and professional concerns, experiences and aspirations. Many colleagues around the world have been a source of encouragement and inspiration and have played their part in helping to keep alive my own sense of the value of music and the importance of music education.

I also wish to pay tribute to the direct and indirect influence of eminent academics who taught at the Institute of Education during the early part of my career. In particular I think of Professors Richard Peters, Paul Hirst, Basil Bernstein and Louis Arnaud Reid, all of whom were important in their respective fields of study and contributed to the thinking of so many people, including the present author for whom they were colleagues. More recently the work of Gunther Kress has also helped to clarify and focus my thinking.

Friends in my own academic department have never failed in their support and I sincerely thank Pauline Adams, Penny Davies, Dr Charles Plummeridge and Dr Robert Kwami. Dr Lucy Green gave invaluable and incisive advice on improving the text before the final version. Jilly Dolphin, our music and drama administrator, calmly maintained communications and managed to keep my in-tray as clear as she could while I was writing. Finally and most important, to my 'extended' family: thank you all for your understanding, unfailing stimulation and support.

Permissions

I am grateful to Henry Holt & Company, Inc. for permission to use the two cartoons by Sempé, *Wladimir Hernsingern and Brigitte* and *André*. Permission to use A. E. Housman's 'Eight O'Clock' has been given by Holt, Rinehart & Winston, Inc. and Denise Harvey & Co. have made possible the use of Cavafy's 'Longings'.

Introduction

This book is for those musicians who think of themselves also as teachers. It is intended for anyone who invents or performs music and for those who may not perform but who respond vitally to music and are inquisitive about its value and function. I hope too that the work may also contribute to the field of the psychology of music, especially if psychologists choose to substitute their formulation 'musical cognition' for my preferred terminology, 'musical understanding'.

In particular, though, the book is intended to inform the theory and practice of music education and help practising and intending teachers. My conception of music education embraces not only teaching in the formal classrooms of schools and colleges and the activities of instrumental instructors. There are many other people who teach music and facilitate access to music without necessarily thinking of themselves as teachers in any formal sense. These include music promoters, composers, performers, programme writers, critics, people in TV, film and radio, organisers of festivals, adjudicators, examiners and those many informal music-makers who, while they may be unattached to institutions, are very active in our communities.

My main aim is to offer a transparent account of the nature of musical experience and to follow through the implications of this perspective for music education wherever it occurs. Obviously, the latter depends substantially on the former: for we can neither teach nor think insightfully about teaching what we do not ourselves understand. The first two chapters of the book are therefore concerned with music itself, with its metaphorical significance and value and with the social dimension of musical discourse. These have always seemed to me to be central issues for all musicians and certainly for music educators.

The central chapter of the book focuses on music education. By way of examples, I attempt to tease out strands of musical experience and set out three fundamental principles for music educators. These principles can assist in developing teaching strategies and help the evaluation of educational transactions, whatever the particular circumstances. Should the reader be wary of the theoretical nature of the first two chapters, it might be a good idea to start with this one and return later to the rationale underlying the principles.

In many countries a political demand for accountability has led to the development of state guidelines, national curricula or 'standards'. Performance indicators and behavioural objectives have replaced intuitive teaching and informal assessment. The effect on teachers has been profound, especially in the organised curriculum frameworks of schools and colleges. The secret garden of the classroom is now open to view and those who work there must show that they are capable gardeners. One consequence is that valid and reliable assessment of students' work has become a vital issue. The fundamental perspective of music as an essential strand of human discourse raises important implications for the practice of student assessment. These are addressed in the fourth chapter.

In the final chapter I consider the relationship of institutionalised music education to informal musical activities in the wider community. Here I suggest some ways in which formal music education in schools and colleges might adapt to a changing world, a situation where rapidly expanding communication systems ensure – to an extent never seen before – that musical discourse has to be seen as a plurality.

The ideas in the following pages are rooted in wide musical experience and also stem from a concern with the practicalities of teaching. A good deal of thought and many years of systematic research underpin what I regard as a 'philosophy' which, though informed by psychology and sociology, is grounded in musical encounters. I owe a particular debt to two major philosophical figures. One of these is Susanne Langer. Her impact on so many people working in the arts and arts education has been profound. The other philosopher is Ernst Cassirer. His *Philosophy of Symbolic Forms* encompasses an imaginative exploration of 'other worlds' than science through a fertile concept of symbolic or cultural modalities (Cassirer 1955).

In recent years it seems that important debates in music education have sometimes been hijacked by writing which verged on pedantry or even personal attack (Elliott 1997; Walker 1998). I have tried to avoid falling into this academic pit. There are more effective and productive ways of engaging with the ideas of other people. An excellent contemporary example in music is the careful review by Wayne Bowman of different philosophical orientations towards the nature and value of music (Bowman 1998). Another and contrasting recent instance is the qualitative empirical study by Patricia Shehan Campbell of ways in which children in a USA urban area use and value music (Campbell 1998).

The musical examples may worry some readers. It is difficult in the medium of written text to convey a sense of musical import. Rather than stay at a general level of cultural or other theories I have attempted throughout to connect with specific musical instances. At times I have attempted this either in descriptions or in staff and graphic notations. There is no attempt to represent the entirety of 'world music', to be somehow culturally inclusive. Indeed that would be presumptuous, for inevitably I am more at home in the music of some cultures than in others. However, the artistic and musical influences, though idiosyncratic, are fairly wide and include eastern and western traditions, popular music and music of Papua New Guinea, South America and Africa. Of course, music is not all the same. Cultural and personal differences will account for many variations of musical type and social function. But most people from most cultures seem to share a propensity to music, just as they share a propensity to language. The focus of this book is what I call the 'space between' and especially the fundamental processes involved when people engage with music. Since I happen to believe that these processes are deep structures, it hardly matters which music is being explored, provided that there is a sufficient range of examples. Thus, should the music examples appear somewhat eccentric, so be it.

I have tried to be as lucid and succinct as possible, though without glossing over controversy. Accordingly, I have resisted dragging into the scene every available protagonist, although I believe I have engaged honestly with several important contemporary issues. Rather than litter the text with detailed and heavily footnoted argument, I have referred the interested reader needing more evidence and persuasion to more substantive publications by citing them in the text. As presented here the thesis is stripped down to what I regard as fundamentals. In this sense it may therefore be considered an *essential* (though not an essentialist) philosophy of music education.

This book is a distillation of many years of teaching and research in the field of music education. I hope that readers will find both development of earlier work and new perspectives here. One ambition has been to convey something of the directness of musical encounters and address the reality of teaching. The perspective is therefore a very individual one and accordingly, the style of writing is not severely academic but deliberately personal, sometimes anecdotal. My intention is that these stories, these vignettes, will illustrate and illuminate the main thesis and help to connect the central concept – that music is a form of discourse impregnated with metaphor – with the actualities of making music and teaching music.

Chapter 1

Musical value

It so happened that, while I was working for a few days in the Sibelius Academy of Music in Helsinki, I found myself invited by the management of my hotel to a reception. The group consisted mainly of business travellers from Nordic and other northern European countries. Eventually I fell into conversation with a friendly Finn. She had a combined degree in economics and chemistry and was working from Sweden for a company which makes and sells flavourings for food and drinks. She spoke Swedish, Norwegian, Finnish, English and recently had begun to learn Estonian to help her sell her products in a region of Europe where she saw a promising new market opening up.

After a while I tentatively asked where she stood in relation to contemporary economic theory. She said she believed essentially in market forces. I wondered aloud how, for example, young children or sick and very old people fit into a world where they may seem to have little if anything to offer in the marketplace. She maintained that we all have something to sell and as an example spoke of her grandmother who is able to recount her family history and is especially illuminating on how things were with the family during the Second World War. In the view of this economic chemist even people who are very ill or those who can hardly communicate at all can teach us something about being a human being. I was very impressed. This is obviously a concept of a market not only for material products and services such as banking and insurance but also where *ideas* and *relationships* are commodities at least as valuable as apples and potatoes, motor cars and apartments.

It did not occur to this businesswoman to think for one moment that her job was unimportant or, indeed, that mine was, though I felt mine was nowhere near so clear-cut and useful as hers and any outcomes from my job were far more nebulous. Her attitude, though, was totally positive. We *all* have goods to trade with others and we are part of the market system, part of life.

What are those of us who work in music or music education to make of this? Of course, music can enhance the profile of a school, college or other organisation. Music can be pleasurable, it can keep people off the streets, it can generate employment, it can enhance social events. But by themselves these reasons are not enough to justify music in an education system. Nor do they provide a rationale for teachers or other musicians who know that what they do is significant, but don't know how to articulate what it is that makes music worth doing.

There is an important issue here. I want to argue that music persists in all cultures and finds a role in many educational systems not because it services other activities, nor because it is a kind of sensuous pleasure, but because it is a symbolic form. It is a mode of *discourse* as old as the human race, a medium in which ideas about ourselves and others are articulated in sonorous shapes.

I intend to use the word 'discourse' throughout this book in an everyday, non-technical sense. Associated terms include 'argument', 'interchange of ideas', 'conversation', 'expression of thought' and 'symbolic form'. And discourse manifests itself in a variety of ways, not only through words. For example, Gunther Kress and Theo Van Leeuwen have demonstrated the existence of a grammar of visual design (Kress and Van Leeuwen 1996). In their quite different ways others have attempted to show how music functions as a symbolic form (for example, Cooke 1959; Goodman 1976; Langer 1942; Nattiez 1987/1990). Discourse continuously modifies the symbolic form in which it appears. Take for instance the daily extension and evolution of languages evidenced in the rapid revision of dictionaries. And discourse can appear in new or fresh combinations of symbolic forms, such as film, television and internet publishing. Discourse is a useful generic term for all meaningful interchange. It encompasses the trivial and the profound, the obvious and the recondite, the new and the old, the complex and the simple, the technical and the vernacular.

As with any other medium of thought, musical discourse can be socially reinforcing or culturally provocative, soporific or challenging. Understanding arising within musical discourse, as in any symbolic form, can be illuminating and rewarding. Many people recognise that music augments the quality of human life and would not wish a day to pass without it (Storr 1992). And this is not simply a sensory pleasure, like eating a banana or taking a shower. Music is part of what Oakeshot calls the skill and partnership of conversation (Oakeshot 1992). For those on the inside of this conversation, such experiences can at times be powerfully insightful. Musical engagement 'speaks of perfection' (Paynter 1997: 15). As discourse, music significantly enhances and enriches our understanding of ourselves and the world. No wonder music is so often interwoven with dance and ceremony, with ritual and healing, and why it takes a central role in celebrating significant life events: birth, adolescence, marriage, death.

At times music has the power to lift us out of the ordinary, to elevate our experience beyond the everyday and the commonplace. For many people music gives rise to what have often been called 'aesthetic' experiences. But what kind of experiences are these? And how can musicians and teachers help audiences and students towards the possibility of such 'perfection'? These are important questions. For unless we have a clear vision of the potential nature and significance of music it is unlikely that our performance and teaching will come to very much.

My first task in this book is therefore to uncover some of the foundations of musical experience. In order to do this it is necessary to clear some ground through the jungle that has sprouted around the idea of the 'aesthetic'. I have no intention of attempting to negotiate its sprawling and controversial literature. However, it is necessary to attempt some clarification, since 'aesthetic' and 'artistic' are words often uttered in the same breath.

The aesthetic and the artistic

The aesthetic tends to be defined in a multiplicity of ways and is very often an unsatisfactory confusion of several different concepts, including the aesthetic, the artistic and the affective. For example, Bennett Reimer sees the aesthetic, artistic and intrinsic as interchangeable (Reimer 1989: xiii), while Peter Abbs views aesthetic experience as those encounters which are highly memorable or overwhelmingly affective. If we take the view that there is a special kind of experience called the aesthetic then we are likely to push all the arts together into this overall category. This is so for Peter Abbs who advocates the idea of a 'generic community' of the arts. This aesthetic community has three shared characteristics that distinguish it from other areas of human activity (Abbs 1994: 92).

1   All the arts 'create forms expressive of life'.
2   All for their meanings 'depend upon their formal constructions that cannot be extracted or translated without significant loss'.

3   They require 'not a critical response but an aesthetic response – a response through feeling, the senses, and the imagination'.

Thus stated, the problem becomes fairly clear. The first of these defining statements must surely apply to *all* forms of discourse unless a very restricted meaning is placed upon the phrase 'expressive of life'. Science and philosophy, for instance, also create meaningful expressive or communicative forms. The second statement may appear to be more artistically distinctive but is also true of interpersonal relations, sexuality and humour, in fact of all intuitive or holistic ways of taking the world. And I suspect that much advanced thinking in mathematics might also depend on 'formal constructions'. The third statement containing the idea of aesthetic response seems more easily justified, even if the argument is somewhat circular. Even here though, it is difficult to imagine artistic participation, let alone teaching the arts, which is divorced entirely from critical awareness. In any case, is this aesthetic response through the senses not also characteristic of eating, drinking, participation in games and in the enjoyment of nature? So it seems that all three of Abbs' allegedly distinctive 'aesthetic' characteristics appear to be shared with several other forms of symbolic discourse.

There is a related difficulty in that aesthetic experience itself is often thought to include appreciation of non-artistic phenomena. The play of light on water, a golden sunset, a fine shot in a ball game, an elegant experiment, a tight argument: all these may qualify as aesthetic. Malcolm Ross stretches the concept even further until it becomes a kind of generic life-force.

> A good aesthetic education, a healthy aesthetic development, will, by definition, increase the life-force, empower the life-drive, release all our instincts to savour life and live life to the full. It will be strengthening – virtuous.
>
> (Ross 1984: 65)

For Ross aesthetic education is not an induction into what he calls the 'artistic predilections of a privileged social minority' but has to be a much more inclusive activity. In his ideal conception:

> The classes would be jam sessions and the public events community happenings. Arts lessons would generate an artistic dimension in the school's life – not merely function as yet another variation on an academic or vocational theme. There would be room for cartoon, comic strip, food, film, make-up, D.I.Y., clothing, the fairground, muzak, Boots Art, pop, electronic games, cars, bikes, hair, graffiti,

advertising, entertainment, politics. The esoteric practices of the studio, the theatre, the concert hall, the gallery would be replaced by an altogether more robust, more plebeian, more ephemeral range of activities – all imbued with what I have called the vernacular spirit (46).

An emphasis by Ross on the virtues of day-dreaming, cordiality and the vernacular is in direct opposition to contemporary educational 'standards', learning objectives, vocational attitudes, education as preparation for work, 'school to work' programmes, the division of the timetable into 'subjects', student assessment and all the other baggage and clutter of the school and college curriculum. I would guess, though, that even in the context of our contemporary educational institutions, we would all want to promote *eventfulness*, if only as an antidote to the low-intensity sequences of dull routines that so often seem to characterise the educational 'basics'. It would certainly be very stimulating, affirming and encouraging for arts teachers to see themselves within this kind of frame, as important initiators of aesthetic experience, setting up celebratory activities that illuminate every corner of life, launching events that vitally pulse through the formal curriculum and resonate throughout the communities of schools and colleges. We are all surely on the side of the aesthetic rather than its opposite, the *anaesthetic*.

The main problem of special pleading for the arts based on the supposed unifying idea of the aesthetic is that it reactivates the underlying old and unhelpful division between the 'affective' and the 'cognitive', between feeling and thinking. This dichotomy is, of course, false. As John Dewey reminds us: 'The odd notion that an artist does not think and a scientific inquirer does nothing else is the result of converting a difference of tempo and emphasis into a difference in kind' (Dewey 1934: 15).

During the late 1990s the 'aesthetic' became something of a battleground among music educators, especially those in North America. The idea of music as aesthetic education had previously been articulated most consistently by Bennett Reimer, though he defines aesthetic very differently from Ross (Reimer 1989). Among others, David Elliott felt the need to counter this and he advocates the demolition of this deficient philosophy which, he believes, is characterised by four common, basic and profoundly wrong assumptions:

- that music is a collection of objects or works;
- that these musical works are for listening to and that there is only one way of listening, aesthetically and with attention to the structure of the work;

- that the value of these works is always intrinsic, internal;
- that if we listen correctly to these pieces we may achieve a distinctive aesthetic experience.

(Elliott 1995: 23)

Obviously, this list represents a very limited view of what music is all about and the uses to which music is put. Unfortunately though, it is a caricature of the views of Reimer. Elliott also manages to misrepresent several other writers whom he clusters together as promoters of the 'aesthetic concept of music education', including, I have to say, the present author. It is not my intention to enter this fray, indeed this particular debate can be seen as something of a side-show, offering very little to our understanding of the nature of music or the priorities of music education. Furthermore, neither side of the argument seems to be based on any systematic study of how people actually make and respond to music, let alone teach it. However, we ought to notice one important feature arising from this aesthetic/artistic wrangle.

Elliott seems to confuse the aesthetic with what has been called formalism. On this view, musical meaning and our response to music is associated mainly with internal structural relationships (Meyer 1956). So when involved with a particular performance we build up a set of expectations, in western music perhaps to do with melodic or harmonic direction or with the repetition of metric rhythm patterns. Our response to the music is thus bound up with our predictions, what we are led to expect is going to happen and the tension or release that is generated by what *actually* happens. This is certainly part of the story and we shall return to it later. However, I would disassociate myself from any extreme version of such a theory. Indeed, in an earlier book I was critical of the limitations of this formalist view.

> The problem is that it fails to connect musical experience with other experience in any direct way. Music has once again been removed from life, turned into a kind of game, if of an intellectual kind. It seems more likely that expectation and surprise are part of the *mechanism of engagement* with the work. It is how we are kept interested and involved, is how we are brought into action with prediction, speculation and ideas about what is happening and what is likely to happen, and in all this there is obviously likely to be a trace of excitement. But it is *not* the prime source of high aesthetic pleasure. The peak of aesthetic experience is scaled only when a work relates strongly to the structures of our own individual experience, when it calls for a new way or organising the schemata, or traces, of previous life events. This experience of seeing things by a new light is called by Koestler

'bisociation'. It is a 'eureka' experience, what Langer calls the triumph of insight: we discover in the work a 'point of view' that seems to us at the moment to be a kind of revelation.

(Swanwick 1979: 36)

If this is what Elliott means by 'distinctive aesthetic experience' then I certainly plead guilty to finding it desirable. The important point, though, is that the 'aesthetic' is but *one* element of artistic activity (Best 1989; Reid 1986). As Abbs himself affirms, the arts are symbolic forms, they are shared systems of meaning, what I am calling discourse. They develop within particular traditions. And Meyer is right: music inevitably involves *cognitive* elements, among these being proficiency in making connections and comparisons, the facility to 'read' established musical conventions and the ability to recognise and respond to deviations from expected musical norms.

The processes of metaphor

As we have seen, one weakness in the idea of the aesthetic seems to be that it separates out music and the other arts from other forms of discourse, isolating it from other achievements of the human mind. But rather than try to find a distinctive role for the arts in general or music in particular it seems to me far more profitable initially to ask the question: what does music *share* with other symbolic forms? Music is not some curious anomaly, split off from the rest of life, not just an emotional thrill by-passing any processes of thought, but it is an integral part of our cognitive processes. It is a way of knowing, a way of thinking, a way of feeling. Of course musical activity is in certain respects unique. It does a special job that words or visual images find less congenial and often impossible. But it is not totally cut off from other aspects of the human mind, tucked away in some remote area of our nervous system, detached from other ways of having ideas. There are generic psychological characteristics of discourse and these have been clearly identified by, among others, the psychologist Piaget (Piaget 1951: 238–9). These four elements are not necessarily in an invariant sequential temporal order but together they are a useful gloss on my definition of discourse, whether scientific or artistic. In essence they are as follows:

- We internally represent actions and events to ourselves; we *imagine*.
- We recognise and generate *relationships* between these images.
- We employ systems of signs, *shared vocabularies*.
- We negotiate and *exchange our thinking* with others.

These interleaving elements characterise thought and production in the arts just as much as in philosophic deliberation, scientific reasoning, or mathematical thinking. When painting a picture, improvising music, dancing or refining a poem we translate experience into particular images, we bring these images into new relationships and we articulate our thinking within systems of signs, engaging in what Oakeshot calls 'conversation'. Even so, listing the elements in this static way, though helpful in showing something of the commonalities of discourse, does not tell us very much about how discourse is produced, sustained and developed. Nor does it account for our motivation to engage in the 'conversation'. My thesis is that *the dynamic phenomenon of metaphor* underlies all discourse. It is this central concept that now must be introduced.

There is a large and branching literature on metaphor, including contributions from literary, philosophical, psychological and scientific perspectives (Mac Cormac *c.* 1985; Ortony 1979; Sacks 1979; Wheelwright 1962). Within the scope and size of this book it is neither possible nor necessary to review this work. Instead I shall stay close to those writers who interpret the concept of metaphor very widely, not limiting the definition to a specific literary 'figure of speech'. On this view *metaphor* (not *a* metaphor) is a fundamental generic process. Roger Scruton also conceives of metaphor as a generic term for 'figurative language generally', 'bringing dissimilar things together, in creating a relation where previously there was none' (Scruton 1997: 80–3). In other words, metaphorical processes allow us to see things differently, to think new things. In metaphor two (or possibly more) domains intersect, often unexpectedly and at times with novel consequences.

The word *metaphor* is, of course, evolved from ancient Greek: *meta* indicates time, place or direction while *phéro* means to carry. *Metaphorá* then literally means conveyance from one 'place' to another. The original sense of 'metaphor' is in itself a metaphor. We do not mean that we literally carry things from somewhere to another place but that relocating an image or concept from one setting to another is *like* such a physical action.

A very good example of metaphorical likeness is provided by a colleague, Gunther Kress. A child of three makes a drawing of a car which consists only of a number of circular shapes. 'I'll make a car . . . got wheels'. A car is thus essentially defined by what Kress calls its 'wheelness', it is being represented by images of wheels and images of wheels are in turn represented by signs, circles on paper which communicate to us the child's idea of 'car' (Kress and Van Leeuwen 1996: 6). The process is essentially *metaphorical*: a car is most like wheels and wheels are *most like* circles. This idea of *likeness* is very important for our understanding of how ideas develop (Swanwick 1988: 46). However, metaphor depends also on our capacity to discern *unlikeness*. In a very important way, circles on paper are not really wheels and wheels are not really cars: they are circles on paper. These circles have become *symbols* which can be brought alongside other symbols in new graphic relationships. This ability to generate novelty lies at the heart of discourse. These metaphorical processes are implicit also in poetry, humour and music.

Longings

Like the beautiful bodies of those who died before they had aged,
sadly shut away in a sumptuous mausoleum,
roses by the head, jasmine at the feet –
so appear the longings that have passed
without being satisfied, not one of them granted
a night of sensual pleasure, or one of its radiant mornings.

(Cavafy 1981)

We recognise the presence of metaphor very readily in poetry. In the poem 'Longings', the Alexandrian poet Constantine Cavafy draws an obvious comparison between the young dead and unsatisfied longings. There is also, though, an element of implied positive sexuality and, in the last line, a sense of sunrise, though sadly this will pass unseen by the young dead. Even so, we, the readers, are briefly lifted out of the chilly mausoleum by this alternative image of daybreak and the sombre implications of the words 'not one of them granted' seem momentarily pushed aside by images of 'radiant mornings'. Two things are happening here at the same time. A *likeness* is being implied, a similarity between ungratified desires and early death. But there is also dissimilarity, an *unlikeness*, a contrasting brightness which has the effect of deepening the darker images. The strength of the poem lies particularly in the internal tension caused by juxtaposing things that are *unlike*.

Initially all metaphor contains an element of novelty arising from potentially dissonant relationships, though we can easily come to overlook such anomalies. For instance, when we say 'the wind is biting' we do not usually intend to suggest that the air has sharp teeth or a strong muscular jaw. What we are trying to do is to find a way of describing the distinctively painful kind of gripping coldness that we are experiencing. After repeated use the initial collision of meanings tends to fade and what was once a metaphor becomes a commonplace 'literal' statement. In ordinary conversation we may not even notice the metaphorical origins of such phrases as 'a biting wind' and we are quite happy to speak of the 'legs' of a table, 'attacking' an argument or 'grasping' an idea without any consciousness of the metaphorical history of these expressions (Mac Cormac *c.* 1985).

However, we also find excitement and take some delight in generating, amplifying and sustaining tensions between dissonant meanings. An example of this would be the sustained logical development based on illogical premises that characterises much of the humour of the Goons or Monty Python. There are also the visual puns that permeate cartoon films, for instance, when Tom is chasing Jerry and is knocked out after running into a wall, his eyes may become like rotating fruit machines or his teeth crack like ice and fall out of his mouth.

In 1997 the popular film *The Full Monty* portrayed a group of unemployed steelworkers in Sheffield secretly working up their own striptease dance routine in the hope of making money. In one scene they are in line at the Job Centre, where it so happens a recording is being played of some of the music they have been using in rehearsal. Involuntarily and surreptitiously at first, but then more overtly, they move into their routine, causing some consternation in the Job Centre and a great deal of hilarity among the audience. The novel relationship between the vestiges of a strip routine performed by men in the dismal formality of an unemployment office generates a metaphorical tension which spills over into laughter. Subversion is at hand.

There are, then, two sides to the coin of metaphor. Metaphor carries something we know and which we have already assimilated into a new context, requiring us to accommodate to its relocation. The metaphorical process lies at the heart of creative action, enabling us to break new ground, making it possible for us to reconstitute ideas, to see things differently.

Eight O'Clock

He stood and heard the steeple
Sprinkle the quarters on the morning town.
One, two, three, four, to market place and people
It tossed them down.

Strapped, noosed, nighing his hour,
He stood and counted them and cursed his luck;
And then the clock collected in the tower
Its strength, and struck.

(Housman 1992/1965)

We saw dissimilar elements in the poem 'Longings'. They also lie at the heart of 'Eight O'Clock', a poem by the English poet A. E. Housman. At first sight there appears to be nothing very distinctive in the first stanza, apart from the obvious metaphoorical allusion to the clock 'sprinkling' its chimes over the marketplace, a transposition from an aural to a visual mode. A commonplace rhyming scheme trots out apparently trivial words.

The second verse tells quite a different story. There is the same underlying rhyming pattern as before but new rhythms and hard-edged words tell quite another story. The last two lines gather in tension until the curious and unexpected placing of the final verb, 'struck', which functions as a pun. A pun is one of the simplest types of metaphorical activity, a device in which two worlds meet in a single word. We may even consider a rhyme to be a kind of half pun, where a similar though not identical word-sound bridges two meanings. The easy consonance of 'struck' and 'luck' is ironic, to say the least. We are watching an execution behind a prison wall. When this idea dawns, the significance of the title shifts radically and the first stanza is seen in a new light.

What a metamorphosis this is. In fusing the machinery of the church clock with a hanging in the prison yard it seems as though the religious and legal systems have themselves carried out the sentence. The execution happens impersonally, mechanically, like the striking of the hour. And the second stanza *is* and at the same time is *not* like the first: it is a shocking divergence from what we might expect from the naivety of the beginning and the superficial similarity of the two stanzas. Such metaphoric dislocation takes us beyond the commonplace. A set of new relationships is created out of images we already thought we knew. The effect of bringing together different entities at the same time has been imaginatively explored by Arthur Koestler in his book *The Act of Creation* (Koestler 1964). He does not use the term metaphor but calls the process *bisociation* and finds it at work in humour, the sciences and the arts.

Whatever the terminology, we can see that metaphor is a process capable of producing new insights. Metaphor allows us to see one thing in terms of another, to think and feel in new ways. This is the secret of creative work in the sciences and the arts. It also lets us find things funny. The old joke, 'What's a Grecian urn?', with its music-hall response of '40 drachmas an hour', relies on a simultaneous allusion to two different worlds by way of an ambiguous apostrophe, an uncertainty about the correctness of the word 'Grecian' and an aural pun on 'urn' and 'earn'.

A similar collision of meanings underlies the highly compressed jibe which has been attributed to feminists, 'When God made Man it was only Her first attempt'. The first four words are a common enough sequence from which we might continue in a predictable trajectory. But the last six words break our expectations and turn the communication right round, from a traditional theological image to a feminist universe of meaning.

As Arthur Koestler brilliantly argues, all humour depends on such clashes of different worlds of meaning, sometimes sudden, as is the case with a punch-line, sometimes with different sets of possibilities running alongside over a period of time – as in a farce where there may be a sustained misunderstanding which is known to the audience but not to the characters. As we have seen, the potential excitement of smuggling an idea over a classificatory border may of course vanish in time and with use. We may become so familiar with a joke or an allegedly funny 'situation' that we no longer find it amusing. It may then be said to have lost its metaphorical novelty. Our ability to respond to humour depends on the perceived freshness of the suggested relationship as well as some understanding of what characterises the different worlds that are being rubbed together. Take the story of the person going to a psychiatrist for an assessment:

PATIENT: Doctor, what is your diagnosis?
DOCTOR: In my opinion you're crazy.
PATIENT: That's a terrible thing to say, I want a second opinion.
DOCTOR: Very well, you are also ugly.

The third line leads us to expect something else, perhaps:

DOCTOR: OK, I'll give you the address of another specialist.

The actuality is very different and here we must make an intuitive leap in taking in the unexpected new meaning of 'a second opinion'. Furthermore, psychiatrists are really not supposed to say such things to their patients, even if they often covertly might like to. This joke also suggests a transposition of the overt and covert.

This metaphorical impulse to enjoy new ways of seeing is found in all forms of discourse where lively minds are thinking. I have seen a Japanese woman dancing with a man disguised as an animal. She later told me that she too was supposed to be an animal. I have seen another lady make a gesture of love to total strangers and watched Garrett Kam performing a Javanese court dance where he was a man pretending to be a woman who was herself pretending to be a man. All this took place at a conference on Asian dance and music in Singapore and no one, as far as I know, was arrested.

Here are metaphorical transformations indeed. In such displays of shifting role we are invited, challenged, to reformulate our attitudes to gender, to recall and at the same time to suspend conventions. At the same gathering a choreographer from Thailand, Professor Nasaruddin, spoke of the cutting edge the arts have in breaking out of 'robotic' behaviour. He certainly exchanges new lamps for old, making moving landscapes with people, bamboo and fabrics. In such ways are we able to think the previously unthinkable, sometimes with a sense of shared insight, when, as Wordsworth said, 'we see into the life of things'.

Music as metaphor

I shall now argue that in musical engagement the metaphorical process functions on three cumulative levels. These are: when we hear 'tones' as though they were 'tunes', sounds as expressive shapes; when we hear these expressive shapes assume new relationships as if they had 'a life of their own'; when these new forms appear to fuse with our previous experience, when, to use a phrase of Susanne Langer's, music 'informs the life of feeling' (Langer 1942: 243). Let us see what happens if we listen to a specific composition 'as if' it were metaphor.

R.Schumann.Op.15

Music example 1 Schumann's 'Of Strange Countries and People'

'Tones' are heard as 'tunes'

Because this music is likely to be familiar to western pianists we may not even notice that from the very beginning we tend to hear it as *music* rather than as a collection of separate sounds. Tones become tunes through a psychological process whereby we tend to group single sounds into lines and phrases, hearing them as gestures. In the same way we tend to see alternating lights around the illuminated borders of billboards or shop window displays as continuous lines rather than as separate lamps. I am, of course, using the word 'tunes' very broadly to mean any kind of musical gesture, expressive unit, or phrase, including such examples as the atonal and non-tonal shapes that form much mid-twentieth century 'serious' music, Indian tabla playing and African drumming patterns. Even a single tone can be heard as a phrase, such as the 'A' on the trumpet at the start of Wagner's *Rienzi* overture which is perceived quite differently from the 'A' used for symphony orchestra tuning.

Hearing sounds as music requires that we desist from giving attention to separate sounds and experience instead an illusion of movement, a sense of weight, space, time and flow. Normally we do this very easily, except when the music is very unusual for us or when we are required to listen in a pre-metaphorical mode, as when tuning or otherwise regulating an instrument. We can, of course, choose not to listen for 'tunes' and instead name single sounds, chords or intervals, as for instance when writing from dictation in a conventional aural training session. However, we cannot climb through this kind of technical analysis towards any sense of line or motion. Even when a wider view of aural discrimination is taken than pitch and rhythm materials (Pratt 1990), no amount of analytical skill with intervals, durations and timbres gets us to experience whole shapes. In fact it can divert us from hearing sounds as *if* they were lines and motion.

How tones become tunes depends to some extent on performance decisions, involving choice of speed, weight of sound, accentuation, balance between the various components and other elements of articulation. It also involves a particular interpretative stance on the part of the listener. On one such interpretation the beginning of 'Strange Countries' may appear to float forward, impelled onwards by the arpeggio accompaniment. The top line is song-like and the bottom part sings a mirror image. A quiet, smooth, unhurried but flowing performance can give a sense of ease and openness, a feeling of effortless, even dream-like motion. Descriptions of this kind are obviously both arguable and inadequate, but they may give a rough idea of one possible interpretation. Is this dream-like quality somehow related to the foreignness intimated by the title? The piece is certainly not a pastiche of supposedly 'exotic' music.

And these qualities are 'likenesses', not a direct copy of feelings or events: they are a *resemblance* rather than a reproduction. As Donald Ferguson says, musical metaphor consists in a 'transfer of the behavior-patterns of tone into the behavior-patterns of the human body' and motion and tension is the basis of musical expression (Ferguson 1960: 185). This process has been noted by many writers, including Roger Scruton who also believes that music involves 'metaphors of space, movement, and animation'. For him music is an experience that has 'sound as its object, and also something that is not and cannot be sound – the life and movement that is music' (Scruton 1997: 96).

The curious thing is that when we are engaged with music as audience-listeners we may overlook this metaphoric process and remain unaware that there is a dynamic relationship between sonorities and expressiveness. Not so for those involved in musical production. They know that part of the process of musical discourse lies in attending to the reality of sounds and to vocal and instrumental techniques, while simultaneously being conscious of the illusion of expressive gesture.

'Tunes' are heard together in new relationships

The second level of metaphor depends upon internal relationships which are constantly changing and evolving. Concentrating now on expressive shape, at the start of 'Strange Countries' – the first five melody notes – the melodic line reaches up and then floats down. But at the same time the bass stretches down and then glides upwards, almost a mirror image of the top line. This opening up of space in this way between the outside parts suggests a feeling of expansion, a gesture which is immediately repeated. If we are familiar with music of this kind then by the fifth measure we may begin to predict some change. The new chords in the left hand and differences in the right hand confirm this expectation but the effect of extending the phrase length over four measures rather than two is an 'unlikeness' to be savoured.

The second section begins with something reminiscent of the original melody, though now lying in the extreme bass. This is further transformed by transposing the directionality of the previous bass line and treble. In the sixth bar of this second main passage the motion is almost stilled. The texture becomes cloudy and the harmonies ambiguous, all this reinforced by the pause, the *ritardando* and the performance implications of the pedal sign. From these dissimilarities and ambiguities we come again to the first idea, though of course it is the same only on paper. For nothing can be the same after what has gone before.

On this, the second metaphorical level, what we perceive as expressive shapes appear to undergo change by juxtaposition, realignment and transformation.

Carrying with them their affective suggestivity, musical gestures are brought into new relationships. There may be association and realignment of these suggestive images, elements of internal playfulness and musical speculation – in some music, even outright surprise. In the first piece of his *Musica Ricercata* for piano, György Ligeti uses only two tones and their octave transpositions. But the second of these tones occurs only once, at the very end. This feature has all the hallmarks of the final punch-line that characterises so many jokes.

From a different area of musical discourse, John Chernoff notes that Ghanaian musicians 'expect dialogue, they anticipate movement, and most significantly they stay very much open to influence. [. . .] there is always an in-between, always a place to add another beat' (Chernoff 1979: 158). The same fundamental metaphorical processes are at work here as in other music, though this time in a community well adapted to flexible interaction. Sounds are heard clustered as phrases, repeated phrases are further transformed into new relationships.

> The most important issues of improvisation, in most African musical idioms, are matters of repetition and change. [. . .] a drummer takes his time and repeats his styles to allow an interesting beat to continue, or a repeated rhythmic response provides a stable basis to clarify other rhythms which change [. . .]
>
> The repetition of a well-chosen rhythm continually reaffirms the power of the music by locking that rhythm, and the people listening or dancing to it, into a dynamic and open structure.
>
> (Chernoff 1979: 111–12)

This is musical 'form' in an organic sense. Our attention oscillates between resemblances of feeling (the old) and these resemblances woven into new combinations. In this 'dynamic and open' metaphorical process music appears almost to have a life of its own.

Music informs the 'life of feeling'

There is yet a third metaphorical shift that goes beyond hearing sound materials 'as if' they had expressive shape and these realigned gestures 'as if' they had an independent existence. This third transmutation gives rise to the strong sense of significance so often noted by those who value music. This almost magical quality of experience has attracted a variety of names, some of them problematic, including that of the 'peak experience' and 'aesthetic emotion'. Csikszentmihalya calls it 'flow', and believes that through such optimal experiences we develop 'sensitivity to the being of other persons, to the excellence of form, to the style of distant historical periods, to the essence of unfamiliar civilizations. In so doing, it changes and expands the being of the viewer' (Csikszentmihalya and Robinson 1990: 183).

Whilst castigating those he believes hold to the universal and unique quality of aesthetic experience, David Elliott subscribes with approval to this idea of 'flow'. 'Flow' is even thought to occur across different activities and cultures (Elliott 1995: 116–17). It is itself seen as a universal. 'Flow' is characterised by a strong sense of internal integration, by high levels of attention and concentration and – at times – complete loss of self-awareness. Similarly, aesthetic experience is seen as 'intrinsic, disinterested, distanced – involved, outgoing, responsive [. . .] absorbed by and immersed in' (Reimer 1989: 103). 'Flow' is really just one more attempt to describe and evaluate those experiences which seem to lift us out of the ruts of life and which have been variously called transcendental, spiritual, uplifting, 'epiphanies', yes, and *aesthetic*. So let us not quibble over what we want to call such experiences, but acknowledge their existence and try to understand how they occur and what their value might be.

Musical 'flow' arises *when all three levels of the metaphorical process are activated*. Then even experience of music as simple and well-known as 'Strange Countries' can be truly 'moving', 'affecting', 'e-motive'. Whether we want to call this 'aesthetic experience' or 'flow', these peak experiences give music a special place in virtually every culture. Writing of participation in Ghanaian music, Chernoff has little doubt about the fusion of music with the life of feeling.

> In music, the contrasting, tightly organized rhythms are powerful – powerful because there is vitality in rhythmic conflict, powerful precisely because people are affected and moved. As people participate in a musical situation, they mediate the conflict, and their immediate presence gives power a personal form so that they may relate to it. [. . .] In limiting and focusing absolute power to specific forms, they encounter power as a reality which is not overwhelming and devastating but strengthening and upbuilding.
>
> (Chernoff 1979: 169)

Remember Roger Scruton's definition of metaphor, 'bringing dissimilar things together, in creating a relation where previously there was none' (Scruton 1997: 80–3). In Chernoff's account the relationship seems to be between chaotic, arbitrary and pressing feelings and the unifying, consequential and distancing form of music which transcends the immediate.

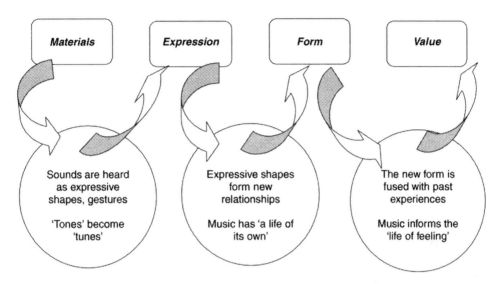

Figure 1 Metaphorical transformations

At this point it may be helpful to consider Figure 1 which is an attempt to summarise in pictorial form the three metaphorical processes implicit in musical experience. The lower level of Figure 1 is of course invisible, unobservable. The psychological processes that constitute metaphorical transformations are hidden from view. But we have evidence of their existence in musical activities and in what people say about music. Out of the hidden processes of metaphor arise four observable layers. These I call *materials, expression, form* and *value*. I have elsewhere advocated the consideration of the inter-relationship of these four layers as a fertile way of thinking about music and music education (Swanwick 1979; Swanwick 1988; Swanwick 1994). We can now see that they are the manifestations of essential metaphorical processes, giving rise to a strong sense of music's value.

The significance of music

With all three metaphorical levels engaged, music seems to become deeply interwoven with Langer's *life of feeling*. But how? Here we reach the difficulty of trying to unravel something of music's ultimate value. In the next section I offer just a hint of how we might begin.

Of all the arts music is the most abstract while drama is perhaps the most obviously 'representational'. By representational I mean there may be much more of an obvious connection with our lives and the lives of others as they are 'played' before us. At the same time we can enjoy the metaphorical transformation of life events to some extent distanced within the framework of theatrical conventions and dramatic processes. But what in music is the equivalent of these life events? The answer seems to lie in music's potential to suggest virtual weight, space, time and flow. These elements of physical movement are de-contextualised in music. In an earlier book I tried to describe how this happens (Swanwick 1979). All feeling states have their own patterns of activity, their own mix of weight, space, time and motion. We say we feel as 'heavy as lead' or that someone is 'weighed down' with care, or that we feel 'light-hearted' or 'light-headed'. We talk metaphorically of being 'stiff with fright' or 'weighed down with responsibility'. Or we may declare ourselves to feel as 'free as air'.

All our experience leaves a residue with us, a trace, a representation which may not enter consciousness but can be activated in other situations. The schemata of past experiences (in Greek 'schema' means 'form' and in German a related word, 'Schemen', means 'ghost, phantom'). They haunt our nervous and muscular systems. Any new movement, thought or feeling occurs in the context of our personal and cultural history and is made possible by reference to the residual schemata of many similar experiences. Many of these are laid down in infancy, according to Anthony Storr a time of extreme emotional states, and normally beyond recall (Storr 1976).

Just as thoughts and feelings constantly change, grow, decay and merge into one another, so musical patterns also appear to be 'on the move'. The ability of music to suggest this movement without pointing to a designated event or specific situation may lead us – erroneously – to assume that musical expression is somewhat vague and therefore lacking in 'content'.

> The moods that music conveys are of a very generalised kind, being no more than schemata of directly experienced moods, with similar rises and falls, degrees of intensity, surges and insistence.
>
> (Passmore 1991: 289)

'No more than schemata'? It is precisely because of its non-literalness, because of its non-explicit but profoundly suggestive nature that music has such power to move us. Not one but many strands of experience can be configured into one single musical encounter, giving it great significance. Those who are able to respond to music in this way will often speak of an experience that is transcendental, made from but at the same time detached from life experience. Something of the way in which this may happen is hinted at by Terence McLaughlin. He sees the patterns of tension and resolution in music corresponding to patterns or schemata in the brain.

> For now, at least, we can see that certain patterns have the effect of calling up recollections of many similar patterns from past experiences and that these recollections arise from many different levels of personality [. . .] and we find ourselves experiencing a synthesis or fusing of many events, many memories, many of the paradigms of existence. This is in itself a new experience, and one which is very much more profound and stirring than the individual experiences of which it is composed.
>
> (McLaughlin 1970: 108)

Patterns or schemata of 'old' experiences are activated but not as separate entities. They are fused into new relationships. We can thus make an imaginative leap from many old and disparate experiences into a single, coherent new experience. It is this potentially revelatory nature of music that accounts for the high sense of value frequently accorded to it. This, the third and most powerful metaphorical transformation, is shared with all symbolic forms. As William Empson put it: 'whenever a receiver of poetry is seriously moved by an apparently simple line, what are moving in him are the traces of his past experience and of the structure of his past judgements.' Poetry makes an appeal 'to the background of human experience which is all the more present when it cannot be named' (Empson 1947: xv). This is certainly so for music too. And reference to the 'background of human experience' is not just a private affair. By a process of empathy we can to some extent enter the worlds of others.

I have tried to explore the common symbolic processes that music shares with other discursive forms. What differentiates music, literature and the other arts from the sciences is the strength of connection with personal and cultural histories. In science this element runs along, so to speak, in the background rather than as the prime object of attention. In the arts this web of feeling becomes a central focus. I have tried to show how this happens through musical performances that connect with mainly hidden traces or schemata of our lives through the deliberate exploration and exploitation of metaphor.

It may be that for some people musical experience that enters the third level of metaphorical transformation may be quite rare. But such an event occurs sufficiently often to ensure that music is traded in all the 'marketplaces' of the world. Musicians and music teachers certainly have something of value to sell.

Chapter 2

Music as culture: the space between

En route once between Boston to Buffalo, I stayed for a couple of days with a former student and her family in Saratoga Springs. On the first evening we sat talking. After listening for a while one of her teenage daughters said suddenly, 'Mom, do I have an accent?' My inclination was to make a joke and say yes, she certainly *did* have an accent and that the only person present without any accent was me, the visitor from England.

We tend to overlook distinguishing features of our own culture, often remaining unaware that in certain respects we even *have* a culture. There is a story – believable though probably invented – of an American Indian who spoke five languages. He correctly believed them all to have a grammar, except one, the language he learned as a child at home, his 'mother-tongue'.

Only when provoked by encounters with cultural practices from elsewhere are we likely to pay attention to 'accents', including our own. In the same way, we notice how our towns and countryside look when we have spent some time elsewhere, perhaps on holiday or working abroad. 'Oh, isn't it green', we say from our seat on the plane, as we approach the waterlogged fields around London's Gatwick airport on the way home from sunny Spain.

These observations help to bring into view two important truths. One is that customs and conventions differ. The other is that exposure to other cultures helps us understand something of our own. Musicians too all have their 'accents'. In this chapter I hope to tease out some of the issues for music and music education that are raised by cultural variation.

We all have an accent

The university marching band was playing at the ball game, though only a version of 'The star-spangled banner' in a stationary position played at the opening and one short number during the seventh innings break. By the end of the game the band folk were really keen to play some more, and to march. So they organised themselves outside the dome. The drummers got there first and rhythmically signalled their whereabouts and in no time the whole band was in position surrounded by an ecstatic crowd. The band director kept a low profile and students themselves seemed to be involved in making decisions, though within the context of obviously well-rehearsed routines.

As it happened, most of them were not music students and it was not a strictly musical event, but they were doing musical things. They were certainly transforming tones into tunes and these musical gestures were reinforced in their stepping, in the sliding and the swaying. There were also some speculative surprises as phrases were broken up and re-assembled. Novel ways of ending – musical punch-lines – were delivered with panache. Bobbing and weaving as they played, stepping forward and backward, flashing instruments up and down: the band moved, the music moved and we too were moved.

It is obvious that all music arises in a social context and that it exists alongside and interleaves with other cultural activities, perhaps as a peer-group bonding agent, or maybe assuring us of the continuity and value of our cultural heritage – whatever that might happen to be – or providing a bit of fizz at a ball game. I want to argue that, however we choose to use music at different times, for those involved in education music has to be seen as a form of discourse on several metaphorical levels. We therefore may have to see music extending beyond its local origins and the limitations of specific social functions. Music is a way of thinking, a way of knowing. As a symbolic form it creates a space where new insights become possible. As I argued in the previous chapter, this is ultimately why music is significant and valuable. It is a value shared with all forms of discourse, for they articulate and fill out the spaces between different individuals and various cultures.

An important question for us here is the extent to which music is bound up in a social web. Are symbolic forms determined only by relative social values or are they 'universal' languages, perhaps with local accents, but to some extent culturally free-standing? The underlying issue here has a long history which I shall not attempt to trace. The suggestion of universals is implicit in Plato's allegory of the cave (Book VII of *The Republic*). People trapped in their tunnel of immediate sensory experience can see only vague representations, shadows of an ultimate reality. For Plato the only way to real knowledge is through philosophical deliberation. This rarefied activity allows us to comprehend the unchanging, absolute 'forms', the essences that lie behind uncertain and misleading images. Of course, such rarefied knowledge is not for everyone, but only for the chosen élite, for the guardians of the state. Most of us appear doomed to stumble around in the dark without any lamp of certainty. If we take this line, then in music education we would be attempting to initiate students into those musical works that embody eternal values.

One alternative to this stern perspective is the 'praxial' view. This also has a long history stretching back probably as far as Aristotle and the mediaeval 'nominalists'. The contemporary concept of 'praxis' has been deeply influenced by sociology and anthropology and is concerned with the relativities of social custom and practice. Differing 'accents' are perceived to be equally valid and nothing is essentially good. The question is rather what anything is good *for* in a specific social context. The meaning and value of music can never be intrinsic or universal but lies in what is socially situated and culturally mediated. On this view musical value resides in its specific cultural uses, in what it is 'good for' in the lives of people. Music is 'good', 'right' or 'fitting', depending on how well it works in action, as *praxis*. A 'praxial' approach to music education has recently been put forward as a new philosophy for music education, though, as we shall see later, it is not without its problems (Elliott 1995; Walker 1996).

There is, of course, another way. We do not have to take the essentialist path that purports to lead to universally valid and absolutely certain knowledge. Nor are we obliged to follow the trail towards knowledge that is thought to be only specific to and reflective of a specific cultural group. As individuals we do not feel our way blindly towards some pre-existing 'truth', nor are we inert repositories of local cultural practice. Even if we may not approach universal truths we can at least arrive at some places of negotiation. This is possible only through symbolic processes, through creating and sharing meaning and values. These meanings and values are obviously social products, to the extent that they are 'creations that are formed in and through th defining activities of people as they interact' (Blumer 1969: 4–5). These defining activities happen to be the discourses of language, mathematics, science, art, music and so on. There can be no symbolic interaction without interpreting minds engaging with symbolic forms.

Each individual exists in a particular set of discursive forms deriving from the social institutions in which she or he finds herself or himself. The resolution of these tensions, contradictions, and incompatibilities, provides a constant source of dialogue.

(Kress 1985: 31)

I take it that education is concerned with studying, engaging in and developing these discursive forms, forms which are plural rather than singular. They are not Platonic, essentialist, intrinsic or invariant universals but are constantly evolving, always 'reforming'. Nor are they sets of fixed, socially conditioned actions without the possibility of reflection, reconstitution or resistance. From this perspective we can see that music not only has a role in cultural reproduction and social affirmation but also has potential for individual development, for cultural renewal, for social evolution, for change.

The ethnomusicologist Alan Merriam believes that the 'study of the dynamics of musical change is among the most potentially rewarding activities in ethnomusicology' (Merriam 1964: 319). Under certain conditions change is less likely, for example, when music is locked tightly into ceremonial or ritual. Change may become necessary or be brought about by technological advances, by migration or travel, by the spread of literacy and by economic prosperity or its decline. Merriam recounts that after an eight-year absence he returned once again to study the Flathead Indians and found that one of these people had also been living away from the reservation. On returning to his tribe he had organised a group which became known as the Flathead Ceremonial Dancers. Using some traditional steps but not whole traditional dances, and performing in a manner not entirely unrelated to mainstream American show business, this troupe became something of a commercial success across the United States. 'The potential changes wrought in Flathead musical culture were substantial: new dance steps, new types of song, new "ethnographic explanations" [. . .] all the result of the activities traceable to the impetus of a single individual' (Merriam 1964: 317). We may worry about the authenticity of this kind of cultural revision and we might wonder about the motives of the individual in this case. But the main import of Merriam's observation is clear: cultures are not for ever set in concrete.

The significance of change is also recognised by the social anthropologist Margaret Mead. Writing as an anthropologist about the uncertain role of formal education in the cultures she studied, she tells us that:

out of the discontinuities and rapid changes which have accompanied these minglings of people has come another invention, one which perhaps would not have been born in any other setting than this one – the belief in education as an instrument for the creation of new human values. [. . .] the use of education for unknown ends.

(Mead 1942: 107)

The space between

This sense of 'unknown ends', the space opened up by potential change, is vital to each individual and to all cultures. Indeed, some room for manoeuvre exists even for the simplest forms of life. According to the philosopher Susanne Langer, environment is a relative concept, depending on how circumstances are interpreted and on a particular organism's repertory of possible responses. It 'may or may not react with far-reaching effects upon its surroundings, but in any case it presents some mechanism which filters the impinging influences' (Langer 1967: 26–7). And similarly for Fritjof Capra, although he is writing from a very different perspective, 'the environment only triggers the structural changes; it does not specify or direct them'. In the interpretative act the system, that is to say the individual organism, 'brings forth a world' (Capra 1996: 260).

The idea of interpretation assumes a special significance for the human species because of our production of symbolic forms and our curiosity which drives us to ask questions such as, 'what would happen if?'. We are not driven merely by needs and emotions, nor are we totally regulated by cultural prescriptions, or social roles, by what Herbert Blumer calls 'reference group affiliations'. For Blumer the human being is an organism 'that engages in social interaction *with itself* by making indications to itself and responding to such indications' (Blumer 1969: 14). This social interaction with ourselves and with others is through symbolic discourse. Because of our use of symbol systems we are not merely responders but interpreters. We do not simply react to our environment, whether physical or cultural, but we also reflect upon our experience.

In summary then, we inhabit a world in which we, like any other organism, have repertories of interpretative behaviour. Unlike other species we have highly developed representational systems, symbolic repertoires, forms of discourse. We engage in what Kress calls 'dialogue' and Oakeshot calls 'conversation'. Blumer's terminology for this happens to be 'symbolic interaction' and Capra's is 'bringing forth a world'. The gist of it is that we each have some margin of manoeuvre and this 'space between' is kept open by access to symbol systems and especially by the playful metaphorical possibilities of artistic discourse. As John Chernoff says of Ghanaian musicians, there is always a place to add another beat (Chernoff 1979: 158).

Of course it is true that all music is culturally rooted, or 'situated' (Elliott 1995). But this does not mean that music is in some way 'uniquely reflective and expressive of a culture' (Walker 1996: 11). This metaphor of 'reflection' here suggests the lingering shadows of old-fashioned referentialism, where music is seen as symptomatic, with a 'programme' of cultural and political values or of the personal biography of the musician. Metaphorical 'likeness' – in the sense of music being 'like' or replicating society – has to be seen in the context of music also suggesting *dissimilarities*: allowing an element of free play, of speculation, what Lucy Green calls a 'chink of light'. 'It is through the experience of inherent meanings that we countenance that virtual aspect of musical meaning which is in itself free of symbolic content, free of gendered delineation' (Green 1997: 250). As we have seen, in musical experience the possibility of breaking out into the light exists at three levels: at the point where we accept the illusion that sound is expressively shaped, when these shapes are perceived in new relationships and when we ourselves are to some extent changed by musical insights that draw upon and inform our personal histories.

So we have to abandon the idea that music stands in a direct relationship with some kind of socially independent reality, as though it were a kind of mirror. Of course there are often strong connections between the music of particular groups and their life-styles and social positions. But this is not to say that music simply embodies these social worlds. Musical discourse is inherently social, not in the deterministic sense of representing of 'reflecting' society but because any form of discourse depends upon negotiating within systems of shared meanings. Distinctive musical styles are maintained and developed through give-and-take in interpretative communities. A musical performance may thus take place in a cultural context without necessarily being totally determined by a dominant culture, as Peter Martin reminds us.

> Artworks are the product of activities shaped by a constant process of decision-making, of innumerable choices through which their creators imaginatively take account of the likely responses of others. This does not imply that artists will simply conform to such expectations – on the contrary, they may consider their whole purpose to be the challenging or subverting of established conventions.
>
> (Martin 1995: 193)

Far from being merely a mirror, then, a copy of our particular society, musical discourse can also be a window through which we can glimpse a different world. As with all forms of discourse, music bridges the space between individuals and between different cultural groups. Following a long and detailed study of music-making in one British city, Ruth Finnegan notes that although musical enactment indeed arises in a social context it is also 'a unique and distinctive mode through which people both realise and transcend their social existence' (Finnegan 1989: 339). Along with this goes an acknowledgement of the diversity of perspectives among individuals, even within the most tightly bound cultural practices. I too am not afraid of the word 'transcend'. There is nothing mystical or 'essentialist' lurking behind this word. Once in a while a straightforward dictionary definition may keep us from turning a relatively simple concept into an 'ism'.

> transcend: *transcendere* = to climb across, transcend, *scandere* to climb, to rise above or go beyond the limits of, to triumph over the negative or restrictive aspects of, to overcome.
>
> (*Merriam-Websters Dictionary*, 1997)

This is the way I am using the word transcend and presumably how Karl Popper intends it to be taken:

> The incredible thing about life, evolution, and mental growth, is just this method of give-and-take, this interaction between our actions and their results by which we constantly transcend ourselves, our talents, our gifts. [. . .] The process of learning, of the growth of subjective knowledge, is always fundamentally the same. It is *imaginative criticism*. This is how we transcend our local and temporal environment.
>
> (Popper 1972: 147)

John Blacking also observed music transcending local cultural practices and he warns against assuming that what he calls 'sound groups' necessarily coincide with social groups.

> A 'sound group' is a group of people who share a common musical language, together with common ideas about music and its uses. The membership of social groups can coincide with the distribution of verbal languages and cultures, or it can transcend them, as in parts of Europe and the Highlands of Papua New Guinea. Different social classes in the same society could be distinguished as different sound groups, or they could belong to the same sound group even though they might be deeply divided in other respects.
>
> (Blacking 1995: 232)

A similar conclusion has been arrived at by several researchers, including Xanthoula Papapanayiotou in her study of the musical preferences of different age-groups in Greece (Papapanayiotou 1998) and some time ago by Herbert Gans. Rejecting the dichotomy of mass culture versus high art and conceiving instead of multiple 'taste cultures' and 'taste publics', Gans identified several musical value groups. Any individual subscribes to any number of such groups at the same time and may change allegiances over time (Gans 1974).

Take the case of Daniel. He is now a tall 13-year-old. He has kept on steadily with his 'cello lessons in spite of some ups and downs and he really seems to like playing. He shapes his phrases with a strong sense of direction, the bow arm sings out the tones and a vibrato begins to creep into the longer notes. The music he plays is more or less of the past, the usual 'cello studies and arrangements of eighteenth- and nineteenth-century music plus some jazz pastiche and 'contemporary' pieces specially written for young players. It's really enjoyable to play along with him. But now he rediscovers the same guitar he first strummed when he was only four and, adeptly deciphering the fingering chart at the front of a guitar self-help book, he gets three chords up and running, the only problem being in which octave to place his changing voice. Something in this musical exploration is new but something is also transferred from his experience with the 'cello.

The new element is Daniel's strong sense of autonomy. He chooses which tune to work on, decides on the strumming pattern and locates what he thinks is an appropriate idiomatic style, including vocal slides and syncopations picked up during his extensive audience-listening. For him this is 'authentic', that is to say, genuine musical experience. His formal instrumental instruction perhaps has this sense of personal relevance less often. There is, though, some carry-over from the 'cello lessons, including a sense of 'this can be sorted out', a strong feeling for phrase shape and harmonic change and an almost instant comfortableness with the physical configuration of the left hand on the fingerboard of the guitar.

There is no conflict here. Daniel knows that musical discourse comes in all shapes and sizes and he is not going to swap one kind of music-making for another. His knowledge of popular music is extensive and he is often a source of information and – more important – of infectious enthusiasm. His response to music from the nineteenth-century symphonic repertory is often to play whole movements several times on CD. When making his fairly rare visits to the classical concert hall, he tends to sit absolutely still, not in deference to any social convention but because he seems to find intrinsic fascination in orchestral sound, in the large range of expressive gestures and in the structural surprises that unfold in good performances. 'At the end did you hear how the tune on the horns came in upside down?'

Awareness of this kind of many-faceted relationship with music prevents us from making assumptions about musical preferences and values on the basis of identifiable cultural groups. There is continual trading in the marketplace of musical ideas. In this limited sense at least musical ideas *transcend their origin*. Although musical processes arise within specific social contexts they are not trapped within them. This should not surprise us if we remember that experiences are mediated by interpreting minds.

We can, then, agree with Jean-Jacques Nattiez and others that any musical work or performance arises from a particular context (Nattiez 1987/1990). But all music has a *musical* context. Schumann's *Scenes From Childhood* has its roots in the musical as well as the other symbolic worlds from which it came. I have no direct admission to the life and times of Schumann, living when and where he did, but I do have some access to his artistic, musical and literary worlds, to what Nattiez calls the symbolic web. This is why I feel able to interpret and respond to this music. Music itself gives insight into the minds and cultures in and from which it originated.

For these reasons any attempt to explore the functions of music cannot arise from semiotics or cultural studies but must be grounded in the particularity of musical experience itself, in musical 'events' of one kind or another. Although there may be relevant and important ideas in sociological, ethno-musicological and other literatures, the interface between minds and music is the central focus of musical engagement and therefore music education. The space between each of us and between individuals and the world is busy with interpretative discourse. Karl Popper calls this 'World Three', an intermediate world between ourselves and what is not ourselves, a world of theories, theorems, formulae, stories, music, dances, paintings, poems, scientific classifications, mathematical calculations and so on (Popper 1972). This is what I mean by 'the space between'.

The focus of music education

I am arguing, then, that musical discourse, while including an element of cultural *reflection*, also makes possible cultural *refraction*, seeing and feeling in new ways. We do not merely 'receive' culture. We are cultural *interpreters*. A conception of music

The Space Between

The 'space between' is full of
ideas articulated in symbolic
forms: inventions, questions,
theories, books, music, art,
science, mathematics and
other discourses. In this
space we articulate and share
our experience of the world.

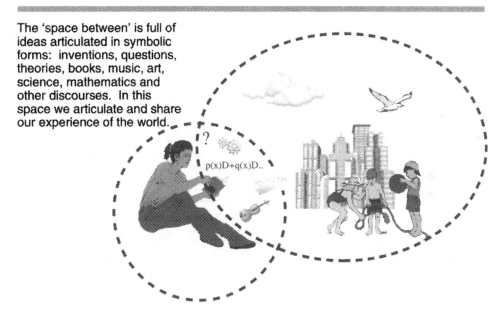

Figure 2 The space between

education as a form of cultural studies or social reinforcement is likely to result in a
very different curriculum from that which identifies music as a form of discourse.
Music teaching then becomes not a question of simply handing down a culture but of
engaging with traditions in a lively and creative way, in a network of conversations
having many different accents. In this conversation we all have a musical 'voice' and
we also have to listen to the musical 'voices' of our students.

This can seem at odds with some educational practice and in conflict with some
theories of music education. Because of their disquiet about contemporary music education in the USA, a number of music educators called an unusual meeting on 1 May
1993. By 1996 this informally organised 'MayDay' group stated its main purpose in
a 'position paper', *Action for Change in Music Education*. The aim was to:

> identify, critique and change taken-for-granted patterns of professional activity,
> polemical approaches to method, and social, musical and educational philoso-
> phies, educational politics and public pressures that have threatened effective
> practice and stifled critical and open communication among music educators.

In this paper a number of what are called 'regulative ideals' were put forward to guide dialogue and promote change. As a member of the group I was asked to comment on and develop the second of these ideals. This runs as follows.

> The social and cultural contexts of musical actions are integral to musical meaning and cannot be ignored or minimized in music education.
>
> Aesthetic theories, with their claims that musical meaning and value transcend time, place, context and human purpose and usefulness, fail to account for the fullest range of meanings inherent in individual and collective musical actions. Such theories fall short of providing an adequate rationale for music-making or music teaching. Instead, all music must be seen as intimately tied to social and cultural contexts and conditions. The theory and practice of music education must account for this situatedness of music and music-making. Music educators must have, therefore, a theoretical foundation that unites the actions of producing music with the various contexts of those actions, so that musical meaning appropriately includes all of music's humanizing and concrete functions.

Several people from the MayDay group and elsewhere responded to this text which was published on a website. Among others, Terese Volk wrote from the Buffalo Public Schools suggesting that the best way to guide students though a plurality of music from different social contexts was to work closely with what she called a 'community culture-bearer'. Mark Turner located the issue of culturally situated music alongside students' perceptions of who the *teachers* are. For him music educators should be 'musicians who have chosen to work and make music with children'. Students will then be more likely to 'accept the musical traditions, situatedness and values we seek to impart. Anyone can teach facts. It takes a musician, however, to impart the essence and inner beauty of our art.' Tom Regelski weighed in with dire warnings against such universal essences and the presumption that aesthetic properties are intrinsic. He urged us to avoid the 'aesthetic thicket' and recognise instead that music is socially situated and socially mediated, that its value depends upon what it is 'good for', that is to say on its 'praxial function'. And several people, including Paul Woodford, urged us not to prolong the 'music-as-aesthetic versus music-as-performance education' debate. This is my own view. There are better places from which to start.

Terry Gates urged us to look again at the many functions of music, especially those set out by Alan Merriam, who had earlier identified and categorised ten general musical functions in society (Merriam 1964: 219–27). This suggestion is helpful and reminds us that everyone uses music in their particular way. Merriam reminds us of the variety of purposes which music is 'good for'. In his own ordering these are as follows:

Emotional expression
Aesthetic enjoyment
Entertainment
Communication
Symbolic representation
Physical response
Enforcing conformity to social norms
Validation of social institutions and religious rituals
Contribution to the continuity and stability of culture
Preserving social integration.

These categories are indeed helpful. In her sensitive study of the ways in which children use and think about music, Patricia Shehan Campbell found that their uses of music ranged 'from the playful to the serious, and from the solitary to the social' (Campbell 1998: 175). She found a good fit between the various musical worlds of the children in her study and Merriam's list. Music does indeed at different times have these various functions and it is up to people to decide for themselves what music is 'good for'. However, the functions of music education are somewhat different from the functions of music, an important distinction which I hope shortly to clarify. Furthermore, Merriam's list is a mixed bag. We ought to notice that there are at least two different types of function here. Following Langer, I shall distinguish them respectively as *signs* and *symbols*.

Signs and symbols

Signs, and the branch of signs we call signals, point to something, stand for something, identify something or (as signals) simply elicit a reaction. For example, a flag or national anthem may be a sign of national allegiance. A red cross or a red crescent are signs of a humanitarian mission. Signs are often symptomatic: a pain in the chest may be a sign of a heart attack, clouds may indicate coming rain. A pistol shot may be a signal to start a race. A particular song may signify peer group solidarity, as at a football game or among a party of teenagers. A greetings card or a bunch of flowers may be a token, a sign of affection.

By themselves signs have limited communicative and metaphorical possibilities.

They tend to be locked into particular situations and usually elicit fairly predictable responses. We do not think *with* them, they do not encourage reflection but may trigger immediate action, as is the case with certain bugle calls. But signals can be taken up into the vocabulary of symbolic forms, as indeed are bugle calls in Britten's *War Requiem* and Mahler's *Des Knaben Wunderhorn*. They then become part of discourse. For instance, the rhythms played on the large lambeg drums that are used at Protestant gatherings in Northern Ireland are straightforward signals of the solidarity of the Orange Order. They bring about predictable – if very different – reactions among Protestant and Catholic communities. But in the novel *Grace Notes* by Bernard MacLaverty, the belligerent sounds of these same drums become symbolic as they engage with other musical ideas in the context of a fictional new composition. As forms of discourse, the arts can raise signs and signals to the level of symbolic forms. Take another example. One ancient signal of departure at sea is the receding sail of a boat. This sign of 'going away' has been taken up by a group of Australian Aborigines in a dance of farewell, where they wave triangular flags which stand symbolically for sails. This transposition from sign to symbol gives more freedom of articulation and greater opportunities for invention. Again an example: Bernard Shaw, in his play *Major Barbara*, playfully juxtaposes two common yet related signs in a crisp dialogue between Barbara, the Salvation Army worker, and her father, Undershaft, a wealthy armaments manufacturer. They agree to meet each other in their respective places of work.

UNDERSHAFT: Where is your shelter?
BARBARA: In West Ham. At the sign of the cross. Ask anybody in Canning Town. Where are your works?
UNDERSHAFT: In Perivale St Andrews. At the sign of the sword. Ask anybody in Europe.

In this conversation the conventional signals of cross and sword are transformed into ironic humour with an unexpected formal symmetry pulling against their apparent differences. The exchange is energised by metaphor.

We can now return more critically to Merriam's list of the functions of music. Emotional expression, aesthetic enjoyment (however that might be defined), communication and symbolic representation all might fall within the orbit of symbolic forms. That is to say, to some extent they may involve elements of what Piaget calls internal representation, the manipulation of images, the production of relationships between these images, the creation and development of shared vocabularies and the negotiation and exchange of ideas with others. Within each of these 'functions' there is certainly a reproductive component but there is also the possibility of metaphoric realignment. These symbolic functions have potential both for cultural transmission and for cultural transformation.

On the other hand some of the items on Merriam's list tend to be tied in to more or less closed systems of signs. The purpose of these is to support cultural reproduction: enforcing conformity to social norms, the validation of social institutions, supporting religious rituals, making a contribution to the continuity and stability of culture and to the integration of society. These functional settings tend not to create or encourage metaphoric exploration. It seems therefore inappropriate to confine music education to these functions, important though they may be in certain social settings, unless there really is some 'space' for real discourse. And indeed there might be and it may occur in unlikely situations.

> On TV one Sunday morning in the United States, a black preacher in Washington DC was emotionally elaborating an Old Testament story. At the end of his exhortatory paragraphs the resident group of instrumentalists joined in with and extended the 'Hallelujahs'. At one point the preacher chided the band and asked them not to make such long interjections. The musicians were taking off into musical discourse to the detriment of his own verbal message.

We have only to consider how artists make free with images of Buddha and Christ, how story-tellers and painters embellish tribal histories or how musicians 'do their own thing', as did Bach and his contemporaries when extending and elaborating a simple Protestant hymn tune, Elton John when singing at a posh funeral and the marching band in Seattle when playing internal musical games after dutifully 'servicing' the ball game.

However, many socially embedded musical functions tend to be quite closed, dominated by societal and especially by peer-group expectations. Music education has us attend wherever possible to those activities that have the potential to keep musical processes open *in as many layers as possible*. Of course, it is fine at times to have music function as a background to other activities or for it to be driven by those activities. But in *music education* the main aim is surely to bring musical conversation from the background of our awareness to the foreground. The question 'what is music's function?' is therefore best subordinated to the question 'how does it function'? This immediately gives a critical edge to educational transactions and has us attend to the actual discourse of music itself, not as a set of signals pointing to social origins or as a symptom of the psychology of musicians, but as symbolic form redolent with layered meanings. Teachers would be failing students if they engaged them only in the tightly culture-bounded elements of Merriam's list, although this might be part of what is done. The educational focus has mostly to be on the actual processes of music-making. Only then is it possible to make sense of the context, whether historical, social, biographical, acoustical or whatever. John Blacking was aware of this.

> [F]or an ethnomusicologist a crucial analytical procedure is not so much to fit the music into a social system, but to start with a musical system and then to see how and where society fits into the music. We should consider artistic cognition, and musical practice in particular, as having primary roles in the imagination of social realities.
>
> (Blacking 1995: 234)

Unfortunately for Blacking's 'imagination of social realities', formalised music education tends to create its own *sub-culture* which may be neither culturally authentic nor musically rich. Indeed, it is sometimes hard to see how institutionalised music teaching connects with the world of musical discourse outside. The final part of this chapter will be concerned with this important issue.

The sub-culture of school music

Music education is not problematic until it surfaces in schools and colleges, until it becomes formal, institutionalised. If we want to strum a guitar, get into the plot of a Wagner opera, play a sitar or sing in a chorus, then finding a teacher, reading a book or joining a performing group may be all we need to do. There is no need to form a curriculum committee, produce a rationale or declare a list of objectives. The informal music student can copy jazz riffs from recordings, ask friends about fingering or chord patterns, learn by imitation – 'sitting next to Nelly' – or widen musical experience by watching television, listening to the radio or exploring record shops. Formal instruction may not be necessary, though for some these formal systems may be crucial points of access. For others the contribution of educational institutions to their personal music education will be negligible and could even be negative. For unlike most if not all other school and college curriculum subject areas, in music many desirable and easily alternative avenues of access are open. The accessibility of music from the ends of the earth and high levels of music-specific information technology compete with conventional school activities. One consequence is that students can have very little time for 'school music' and may probably see it as a quaint musical sub-culture. Very early in the twentieth century, Jacques-Dalcroze drew attention to this tendency of music education to detach itself from mainstream culture.

> Before everything else, always make sure that the teaching of music is worthwhile. And there must be no confusion as to what is understood by 'music'. There are not two classes of music: one for adults, drawing rooms, and concert halls, the other for children and schools. There is only one music, and the teaching of it is not so difficult a matter as scholastic authorities are apt to suggest at their congresses.
>
> (Jacques-Dalcroze 1915)

Dalcroze might not have thought the matter quite so simple had he and his students been exposed to the plurality of music which now surrounds us. In principle though he is surely right. School and college music education can become a closed system that leaves behind or gets left behind ideas and events in the wider world.

For example, beginning in the 1950s, the introduction of Orff instruments into school music classrooms resulted in the creation of a musical sub-culture, characterised by decorative *glissandi* and circling *ostinati*, played on specially designed classroom instruments and based on pentatonic materials. This was music designed for children, bearing little relationship to music elsewhere, except when it begins to approximate the Indonesian gamelan. In the late 1960s came the influence of modernism. Teachers encouraged children to become performers and composers of 'texture' pieces and to use repertoires of aleatoric devices, randomised lists of numbers and so on. Pulse, tonality and modally defined pitch relationships were suspended while students made sound collages, recorded 'found' sounds in their environments and constructed graphic scores. The word 'music' was frequently dropped altogether from books for use in schools and the word 'sound' was substituted: for instance, *New Sounds in Class*; *Sound and Silence*; *Exploring Sound*; *Make a New Sound*; *Sounds Fun*; *Sounds Interesting*.

Here was an attempt to begin again, to make a new start without either the historical clutter of inherited classical traditions or the educational difficulty of accommodating popular music traditions, the alternative musical preferences of many students. And here was an opportunity to link up with the attitudinal world

of contemporary experimental composers. Metrical rhythms and tonal pitch relationships were discarded and attention was switched to levels of loudness, texture
and tone colour. But in the evenings – after these distinctive school experiences – the
students went home and played the Beatles and the Rolling Stones, or perhaps they
taught themselves to play the music that really mattered to them where metric
rhythms and tonal tensions were the norm.

> Many teenagers, for instance, elect to teach themselves to play a musical instru-
> ment – the drums perhaps or the guitar. What do they do? They usually know
> already the kind of sound they are interested in. They insist on the right equip-
> ment. They listen to their mentors and try to emulate them, running into
> problems of sound production and control, figuring their own way through
> them, comparing notes with fellow practitioners, following the example of pre-
> ferred models.
>
> (Ross 1995)

More recently, and in an attempt to recognise the reality of this music 'out there', elements of popular music have indeed entered the formal education scene. But in order
to make itself respectable and to become appropriately institutionalised, popular music
has to be modified, abstracted and analysed to fit into classrooms, timetables and the
aims of music education. The impact of the loudness level is reduced, dancing is
impractical and the socio-cultural context is shorn away. During this reductive process
the activity often becomes what Ross calls 'pseudo music'.

Another way of creating a school music sub-culture is more evident in North
America and usually takes the form of the high school band; especially when given over
to marching at ball games with a purpose-made repertoire, uniforms, parade ground
routines and majorettes. There are, of course, shining exceptions, especially if the
main focus of the band director is to teach music 'musically' rather than be lured into
ego trips and public display. So much depends not on *what* is done but on *how* it is
done, on the quality of musical engagement. Even so, on graduating from school and
leaving the band, a large proportion of US students appear to put it all behind them.
In spite of widespread band programmes there appears little sign among adult communities of continued engagement with instrumental music. The same appears true of
choral programmes. The main aim of these classes seems often to get a programme of
music in shape for public performance, rather than provide a rich musical and educational experience. The teaching methods accordingly tend to be very directive and there
may be considerable repetition in rehearsal of a very small literature, often giving rise

to boredom and satiety. The music may become meaningless and the real musical interests of students are likely to migrate elsewhere.

Reservations about performance programmes in North America have been raised by several writers. These include Leonhard and House, Kirchhoff, and Reimer, who warn against placing an overemphasis on performing ensembles and a concentration on technique which works against musical understanding (Kirchhoff 1988; Leonhard and House 1959; Reimer 1989). The relevance of such activities has also been questioned. The band movement, with its old military connections, hardly reflects the contemporary world of music 'out there'.

> The result has been that students spend an increased amount of time performing on instruments that are foreign to the mainstream of music making in this country and abroad. [. . .] The increased emphasis upon marching band and marching band contests has meant that greater numbers of students are leaving high school band programs literally overloaded and burned out. They have been victims of an educational curriculum that has placed its entire emphasis on the short term reward of winning.
>
> [. . .] The marching band is not the only group that stands in the way of students' achieving an aesthetic music education. The jazz ensemble and the concert band have also been guilty.
>
> (Kirchhoff 1988: 265)

This critical stance towards instrumental performance has a long history. Boethius, writing in the sixth century, distinguished between performers and those whom he saw as musically educated.

> But the type which buries itself in instruments is separated from the understanding of musical knowledge. Representatives of this type, for example kithara players and organists and other instrumentalists, devote their total effort to exhibiting their skill on instruments. Thus, they act as slaves, as has been said: for they use no reason but are totally lacking in thought.
>
> (Godwin 1986: 48)

In an attempt to 'situate' the formal music curriculum in relation to what he calls 'viable music cultures', David Elliott urges us to affirm the centrality of performance in music education (Elliott 1995). In taking this position he chimes with most actual practice in North American music education. But as we have seen there is a danger in organising the curriculum around a narrow concept of performing. This tends to be musically restrictive and the constant repetition of a small standard repertoire may become stultifying. Musical decision-making on the part of students can become almost entirely proscribed.

Furthermore, Elliott's concept of performance is too general to really help us understand what it means to make music. He identifies the essential elements of performance as the 'interpretation of a musical design that evinces standards and traditions of practice'. He notes that there is also the transmission of 'cultural–ideological information' (Elliott 1995: 199). But all these things could be said about many activities. There are presumably standards, traditions of practice and ideological information in pornography or torture.

The metaphorical shifts involved in creating and sustaining meaning have already been identified in the previous chapter. In the following chapter I shall deal with essential principles of music education. For now we can say that in any comprehensive scheme of music education, musical processes should be invoked in as rich a way as possible. This could indeed occur in almost any musical activity, however improbable, as we saw in the case of the band at the ball game. So much depends on the actual quality of the musical encounter. Music education in studios, schools and colleges cannot be confined to supporting a single social function. That is too narrow. Nor, on the other hand, should educators substitute a kind of global musical tourism through the CD and CD ROM for direct involvement in specific musical discourse.

But how is this to be achieved? There needs to be radical re-thinking of how time and resources are used. I can only hint at them here and will say more in the final chapter. A music 'class' will be a place where the major activities of composing-listening, performing-listening and audience-listening take place in relation to music over a cultural range wide enough for students to realise that they each have an 'accent'. Smaller groups than whole-class or whole-band or whole-chorus are essential for student interaction, musical decision-making and individual choice. The musical pathways of children and adults alike are many and various. Educational systems have to recognise this diversity. People become musically engaged when they regard the activity as meaningful, as authentic.

In his book *Culture and Imperialism*, Edward Said quotes with approval Hugo of St Victor, a twelfth-century monk from Saxony: 'The person who finds his homeland sweet is still a tender beginner; he to whom every soil is as his native one is already strong; but he is perfect to whom the entire world is as a foreign place' (Said 1993: 408).

There we have it. One of the aims of musicians and teachers of music may certainly be to enhance our 'homeland' – wherever we think that is. And we also want students to feel 'at home' in the wider world.

Papua New Guinea

Outside the clouds drifted over the high mountains. Inside the University of Goroka, on tables in the music room, student teachers were engrossed in cutting up sago stems into manageable lengths. They had rarely if at all seen sago before, since it grows only at much lower altitudes. Working in pairs and following a demonstration by their teacher, with bush knives they expertly made incisions of two parallel lines about a centimetre apart down most of the length of the outer surface of the sago stem. The last couple of centimetres at each end was left undisturbed and made secure with twine. Inserting a knife halfway along the stem they lifted the strip away from the body of the sago until it resembled a small bow without an arrow. A small piece of bamboo was wedged underneath the strip, forming a kind of bridge. A second piece of bamboo was introduced in the same way and it was seen that these two bridges beneath the stretched sago strip created three different lengths of 'string', giving off different pitched sounds when plucked or struck. The students had to decide how best to tune these three notes. And this was quite tricky, for shifting the bridge in one direction affected the length of the strip on either side.

In the space of just over half an hour they had made sago zithers. With these three chosen pitched notes and using short bamboo beaters each pair of students invented and performed a short piece of music. Then came a revelation. Photographs and tape recordings were introduced of distant tribesmen playing sago zithers in a manner that can only be described as virtuosic. The students looked at their home-made zithers, remembered their own musical inventions and found themselves moving along new musical pathways into a part of the culture of their nation previously unknown.

During this misty morning we were to some small extent able to gain access to and sympathise with the musical minds of strangers from a remote place in a country where inter-tribal confrontation and violence seemed never far away.

What so strongly characterises this particular transaction and many other rich educational encounters which I have been involved in or privileged to witness, is not so much the novelty of new musical 'accents' but the three levels of *metaphor* running through the presentation and production of music. Like members of the Seattle marching band at the ball game, for a time these Papua New Guineans became musicians. That is to say, they heard and organised sound materials as *if* they were expressive shapes: they heard these shapes as *if* they had a life of their own and were organically connected: they began to engage with the 'accents' of others, to refresh their perspectives, to feel as *if* 'the entire world is as a foreign place'. This is what comes of teaching music musically.

Chapter 3

Principles of music education

A view of music as a form of discourse impregnated with metaphor has important consequences for music education. Before beginning to tease these out, here is a summary of the main strands of the discussion so far.

Up to this point I have been trying to give a perspective on the nature and value of music and its role in society. I have drawn attention to those features of discourse which music shares with other forms and identified three ways in which music functions metaphorically. Through the process of metaphor we

1   transform tones into 'tunes', gestures;
2   transform these 'tunes', these gestures into structures;
3   transform these symbolic structures into significant experience.

When attempting to describe the third of these transformations, terms such as 'aesthetic experience', 'flow' and 'peak experience' are interchangeable. This strong sense of personal significance occurs frequently enough to motivate many people to put themselves in the way of musical experiences. Furthermore, this third metaphorical shift is only possible when approached through the two previous transformations. Only when tones become gestures and when these gestures evolve into interlocking forms can music relate to and inform the shapes and patterns of our previous life experiences. Only then does the symbolic form of a musical performance become able to be 'mapped' on to the form of human feelings. These metaphorical processes are internal, invisible but we can observe their effects in the various layers of musical activity. I call these layers *materials*, *expression*, *form* and *value*. They will surface again later on.

In the previous chapter I argued that there are other functions orbiting around these central musical processes and these are often tied in with social expectations and cultural transmission. We can choose how and when to engage with music and we all at various times use music for different purposes, including as a background to other happenings, to enhance social events and for peer group reinforcement. However, music *education* is a special case, especially when it is statutory or is expected to form part of everyone's schooling. An education in music presumes that students have the possibility of access to all three metaphorical processes. Only in this way are we able to open up what I call 'the space between', an area of potential psychological freedom.

This, then, is the vision: of music permeating and expanding our minds at every level. Why is it, though, that a vision of what music is, so often gets lost in what music education actually turns out to be? Perhaps it is that music is particularly hard to manage in the relentless schedules of schools and colleges and for teachers to hold on to its nature and value during the long processions of students through private teaching studios. There are also issues of status and resources. As with the other arts, music is perceived to suffer relegation to the corners of the curriculum and towards the end of the lists of spending options. Even so, we have to be sure that we do not lose sight of the fact that, even in the best circumstances, something less than musical transactions may often be taking place. For I have seen music taught unmusically in conditions where time and resources were more than sufficient and I have seen music taught *musically* in unpromising circumstances. This is, of course, not an argument for starving music education of resources but a recognition that resources alone are not sufficient. As well as understanding the essential qualities of music there also has to be a sense of what it is to engage in lively music education transactions. To this end I wish now to propose three simple working principles that, properly understood and taken seriously, can inform all music teaching, whether in classrooms in school and college, in instrumental teaching studios or in less formal settings. These principles have their roots in the basic premise that music is a symbolic form, that it is rich in metaphorical potential.

First principle: care for music as discourse

One aim of the music teacher is to bring music from the background into the foreground of awareness. Whenever music sounds, whoever makes it and however simple or complex the resources and techniques may be, the musical teacher is receptive and alert, is really *listening* and expects students to do the same. The smallest meaningful musical unit is the phrase or gesture, not an interval, beat or measure. In the work of effective educators, including well-known and influential historical figures such as Kodály, Orff and Jacques-Dalcroze, there is never a moment where a phrase (broadly defined) is not assumed, modelled or expected.

The particular teaching method is nowhere near so important as our perception of what music is and what it does. Running alongside any system or way of working will be the ultimate question – is this really *musical*? Is there a feeling for expressive character and a sense of structure in what is done or said? To watch an effective music teacher at work (rather than a 'trainer' or 'instructor') is to observe this strong sense of musical intention linked to educational purposes: skills are used for musical ends, factual knowledge informs musical understanding. Music history and the sociology of music are seen as accessible only through the doors and windows of particular musical encounters. For it is only in these encounters that the possibilities exist to transform tones into tunes, tunes into forms and forms into significant life events.

What follows is an example of one teacher at work, someone who is at least trying to hold in mind this first principle: that we care for music as many-layered discourse. I trust the reader will excuse the personal nature of this illustration and the necessary analytical detail that accompanies its description.

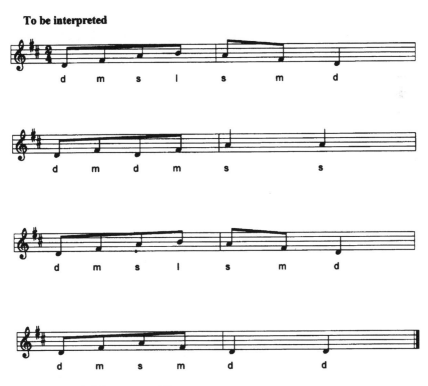

Music example 2 'Mere materials?'

The music shown in Music Example 2 came to mind without any proper invitation. Its arrival was both a relief and a challenge, for I had been asked to be the Keynote speaker at the Organisation of American Kodály Educators (OAKE) in Provo, Utah and I needed to prepare for this event and for an unusual audience. As if informed of my job at the conference, the tune even presented itself to me in sol-fa. And, perhaps not surprising, it also seems to have a slightly Hungarian feeling about it.

There is, of course, nothing startlingly novel or especially subtle about this scrap of music. Looked at in a conventional 'western' way, a major chord seems to be a possible underlying tonal basis. The presence of 'lah' helps to establish the tonal focus and implies an underlying pentatonic scale. It also makes the tune more singable: the stepwise interval between 'soh' and 'lah' helps to smooth out an otherwise angular vocal part. The four printed lines are symmetrically arranged with a repetition between the first and third. We conclude on 'doh' – surely the tonic? The limited vocal range, the short phrase lengths and the repetitions all lend themselves to being remembered and sung by young children. In short: I seem to have unconsciously created or imitated the kind of melody often found in the work of Kodály and among Kodály-influenced educators. Most members of OAKE would, I guess, believe that hearing and singing such an educational exercise helps to establish in our minds crucial interval relationships and a sense of tonality. The square-cut repetitive rhythm patterns are fairly easily read and can be recalled without much effort.

We must remember that any form of musical notation is a form of analysis and that any analysis is necessarily partial and incomplete. To analyse is to take a particular cross-section of wider intuitive experience and narrow our focus to this chosen angle. For example, while walking through a university campus my attention is caught by a striking flowering shrub. During the rest of the walk I then focus especially on the various types of flowering trees and bushes, excluding for a time consciousness of other things, for example, the variety of birds. Homing in on some isolated dimension or feature, engaging in what Polanyi calls 'subsidiary awareness' (Polanyi and Prosch 1975) is what teachers often have to do. It is one way of organising and limiting classroom tasks. It makes teaching manageable. Many curriculum schemes contain attempts to focus activities by recourse to what are often called musical 'elements', for instance, pitch, duration, dynamics, tempo, timbre, texture, and so on. Actually, most of these 'elements' are really sound *materials* and do not involve us in any of the metaphorical levels. This is only one way of analysing musical experience. We have to be careful about this, for by attending to one or two dimensions, perhaps pitch and metric relationships, we necessarily push other things into the background.

Analysis is always in some way a process of reduction and so it is here, in the sol-fa melody. This bit of notation tells us nothing about the potential expressive character of the music. We have no idea about the relative weights of accentuation or of the articulation of the melody; whether it moves smoothly or in a detached way from tone to tone, whether there are vocal slides between notes, whether there are gradations of loudness or speed. And that is fine, as far as it goes. Nothing so sharpens up our sense of tonal relationships as does the sensitive use of a relative pitch system such as sol-fa. Indeed, so attractive to music teachers are such analytical procedures in the layer of sound materials that a whole industry of music ability tests, aural training materials and sequenced instruction has been created – now often computerised.

By themselves these analytical slicings can be constricting. There is a prior state of intuitive response, a way of attending to music that is often driven out by aural analysis, where sounds have potential to become gestures or even cross over between the senses as images. Kenneth Grahame, recalling his own childhood, draws our attention to what he called 'the pure, absolute quality and nature of each note in itself' that is 'only appreciated by the strummer', some notes seeming to be red, others blue or like the sound of bells or armies marching (Grahame 1973, first published in 1895: 75). Nor is it only young children who savour the tonal quality of a single note. Many composers of the mid-twentieth century, including Karl-Heinz Stockhausen and John Cage, attempted to return to this state of childhood grace, insisting that we start afresh from sound itself, freeing ourselves from habitual responses and the limiting conventions of the 'great' traditions.

Hearing sounds as expressive shapes occurs when analytical filtering gives way to intuitive scanning. For it is in such moments of intuitive freedom that the 'space between' is opened up, that the metaphorical leap into expressive meaning becomes possible. If we always or even mostly insist on naming notes and intervals, identifying chords, reading rhythm patterns, and so on, we may get stuck at the level of materials. Probably for these reasons, my small melody began to seem unsatisfactory. For it is quite possible to play it or sing it to sol-fa without any sense of line or flow. What might the tempo be? Should there be any light and shade of loudness? If we get fixated by the interval notation we may find ourselves 'barking at print', just like young children who sometimes read words in a stilted way with little idea of their meaning. Indeed, the assembled OAKE conference at first read these notes in this somewhat mechanical way. But a set of words had previously come to mind, possibly suggested by the rotating feeling of the melody as it moves up and down its anchoring triad. These words begin to be suggestive of a manner of performance, of musical interpretation in the layer of *expression*.

Music example 3 'The possibility of expression'

An accompanying 'drone' now enters the picture and we seem to be embarking on more than just a vocal reading exercise. The repeated onset of the drone clearly marks out the start of phrases and confirms phrase lengths. We get an idea of the arching shapes of the melody from the words and the editorial phrase lines. There is also an implied range of potential effective speed. Any performance of this melody has to be at a tempo steady enough to give a feeling of some size and mass yet fast enough to communicate a sense of rolling, inevitable motion. With words like these the music has to flow forward, though with an impression of weight and size.

This layer of musical meaning, which I am calling *expression*, cannot be experienced if we attend only and always to pitch intervals or rhythm values. These sound materials must be subsumed into a new focus. We may have to forget what we know about 'doh' and 'soh' in order to make the metaphorical leap, to hear a series of previously named tones as an expressive shape. We cannot somehow clamber through pitch intervals to expressive lines. Although tunes are made from tones, exclusive attention to tones diverts us from tunes.

It is important to notice that musical expression is not pasted on as an afterthought. Expressive character is implicit in several kinds of performance decisions, in choosing a tempo, in levels of accentuation, in dynamic changes and in articulation – how the motion from tone to tone is organised. Nor should musical expression be confused with 'self expression'. Musical expression inheres not in our sense of ourselves but in perceiving the character of the music. In the shape of phrases, the flow of tonal patterns and rhythms, changes of tone colour, accent, speed and loudness levels we can find similarities between music's motion and human 'emotion'. As we saw in the first chapter, however, music's expressiveness, while to some extent imitative, is also abstract. It picks up likenesses from life experience, suggestively rather than as an exact copy. Music is a kind of 'virtual reality', often more vivid than 'ordinary' reality. A teacher who is teaching musically understands this and in rehearsal and performance will model and look for expressive shaping in the students' singing and playing. We shall also be looking at each performance holistically, rather than be satisfied with the often necessary but insufficient fragmentation that may occur during rehearsal.

In preparation for my session in Utah the little melody began almost to assume a life of its own. It appeared to have its own evolving *form* and I became an accomplice, an amanuensis in this evolution. Why should we necessarily assume that 'doh' is the tonal centre of gravity? Why not create a small surprise and why not – for the moment – fit it out with new words that pick up this structural change?

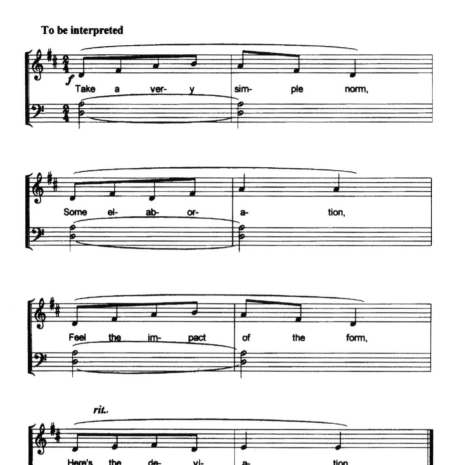

Music example 4 Good form?

The last line is now seen as a deviation set against the background or 'norm' of all that has gone before (Meyer 1956). Now the melody has become even more 'Hungarian' in character and, taken together with the new bass part, turns out to be modal, thus bringing into collision two tonal worlds. Any initial assumptions about the tonal centre are unsettled by this metaphorical shift, by the unexpected twist. The accompanying drone enhances this turn of events and the harmonic shift seems to require some pointing up with a slight emphasis, perhaps with a *tenuto* rather than a slur.

This kind of metamorphosis is the essence of musical form. 'Form' in this sense really has very little to do with larger architectural blocks or idiomatic formulas, such as 'Rondo' or the '12-Bar Blues' but is concerned rather with the unsettling effect of setting up and breaking up expectations. The generalising labels of musical form are but analytical schemes. They draw our attention to overall organising devices. We have to be careful not to confuse these classifications with the organic processes intuitively perceived within each individual piece and performance.

Some time ago on a visit to a Canadian university, I found a small class of students discussing a recently written composition for clarinet and piano whose title now escapes me. They had recently studied this piece and after we listened to the recording they gave their analysis: 'It is in ternary form.' I had heard it differently. The clarinet starts in the lower octave. Fragmentary sounds begin to connect together and assume indefinite small shapes and then clearer and more confident gestures. Throughout this process the instrument works its way upwards towards higher and louder sounds until a longer, firmer melodic line is declaimed. At this point the piano takes over the emergent idea and confidently proclaims it good. This is the high spot, presumably what was thought to be the 'B' section. What follows is a process of progressive fragmentation until we are left with the uncertainties of the low bursts of clarinet sound with which the piece began. Asked what I thought, I said something along these lines. After a while one student said, 'Gee, that's how I used to listen to music before I came to university.'

Dynamic processes cannot be reduced to formulas. We have to be careful not to constrict intuitive scanning by always filtering musical analysis through conventional sieves which let through at least as much as they retain. 'Form' is essentially about *coherence*, about internal *relationships*, about distinctive features; how music holds together, how it engages our attention. As we have already seen, when a joke is free of analytical baggage it is, in its small way, an instance of 'good form', of ideas brought into new relationships, altering our habitual perspectives. Appreciating a joke or responding to the ending of the altered Utah melody is essentially intuitive. Form defined in this way is closely related to what Piaget calls constructional play, where old images are recombined in new ways, metaphorically transformed into new configurations. Responding to musical form is essentially an engagement in this process. The teacher who is teaching music musically is aware of this.

Music example 5 'Value in performance'

Eventually I became quite fond of this small musical creation. It was changing my life! So I worked a little more on it (or perhaps better, *with* it), extending the structure with an almost repeated last line but having yet another harmonic shift that seemed to bring out even more strongly the sense of massive movement implied in the words. The suggested *melisma* and the *ritenuto* on the last appearance of the word 'turning' seems to reflect the effort of this final cosmic 'turn'. If performed with slightly greater weight – more sound, darker tone-colour, *tenuto* – then this final line can have quite powerful expressive and structural significance.

When the time eventually came to attend the conference of the Organisation of American Kodály Educators, I was committed to reaching a controlled, expressively shaped and structurally satisfying performance in which we all might even feel a sense of *value*. Elsewhere I have called this 'meaning for' (Swanwick 1979). *Value* is the fourth layer, an outcome of the third metaphorical shift, where music informs 'the life of feeling'. In the first chapter I referred to this as a new experience arising from a fusion of many past life-experiences. In the space of fifteen minutes or so in Provo, Utah, I think some of us probably made it. A certain sense of delight spread through the hall as the final sounds faded. The music had done its work. This may not have been a 'peak' experience for everyone but for some of us it certainly felt like 'flow' or the 'aesthetic'.

Because of a three-fold metaphorical process, a potentially limiting sight-reading exercise had, for some, become a valued musical experience. In a small way we had the chance to enter a world of musical meaning. We were engaged in musical discourse. The musical teacher always looks for this extension of life's possibilities, plans for the transformation from sound materials to expressive character and for the integration of gestures into form. We also hope (though we can never be sure of this) that students may be 'in-formed' by the experience. This is the ultimate aim of music education.

Second principle: care for the musical discourse of students

Discourse – musical conversation – by definition can never be a monologue. Each student brings a realm of musical understanding into our educational institutions. We do not introduce them to music, they are already well acquainted with it, though they may not have subjected it to the various forms of analysis that we may feel are important for their further development. We have to be aware of student achievement and autonomy, to respect what the psychologist Jerome Bruner has called 'the natural energies that sustain spontaneous learning': curiosity; a desire to be competent; wanting to emulate others; a need for social interaction. We cannot be exempt from understanding what is involved here.

Curiosity is not aroused by dictating notes on the lives of musicians or on social history, or by always telling pupils what to listen for, or by treating a performing group as if it were a kind of machine. There should be some scope for choice, for decision-making, for personal exploration. These include the possibility of working individually and in small groups. Is there any good reason why large performing groups should always function as a collective? Students will bring their own interpretations and make musical decisions at many levels in smaller ensembles. They will begin to 'own' the music for themselves.

Competence is not achieved by muddling through but can be enhanced by sensitively sequenced programmes of study. Of course skills, handling sound materials, are important, but we know they are not the sum total of musical understanding. There are other issues, questions of artistic judgement rather than of right or wrong. What would happen if we played or sang a passage quicker or slower, louder or softer, more or less *legato*? What would it be *like*?

Emulating others suggests having good models: does a student hear others perform or listen to their compositions? Is the teacher a model of sensitive musical behaviour? Would greater recognition of the value of *social interaction* also be a good reason for us to organise more small ensembles than we usually do? Available evidence suggests that much may be gained from teaching instruments in groups rather than exclusive one-to-one (Swanwick and Jarvis 1990; Thompson 1984). Certainly the established practice in Britain and elsewhere of having students compose in groups of five or six, alongside more traditionally organised whole class activities, has extended the definition and range of school music. In these settings various musical 'accents' come alongside each other. Musical ideas and idioms from beyond the classroom are brought together, utilised and evaluated.

Two elements of curriculum organisation can help us respect the musical discourse and individual differences of students. The first of these is the idea of integrated musical experiences. We saw in the previous chapter how Papua New Guinea students entered into a new musical world by making and playing sago zithers. Their response to the recordings of musicians from a remote tribe was a mixture of curiosity and admiration. This strange music began to 'make sense'. We were all able to take an imaginative leap into this highly specialised form of musical discourse because we had ourselves been involved in making and playing sago zithers. Linking the activity of composing (defined very broadly and including improvisation) with performing and audience-listening also allows different students to excel in different ways. One of the Papua New Guinea group was particularly inventive on his newly made sago zither. Another found the new perspective on music in his own country of particular interest and value. Others became more confident in their own composing.

Furthermore, each curriculum activity offers differing possibilities for decision-making, itself a crucial feature of student autonomy. Different activities offer different types of musical possibility. Performing in very large groups offers very little scope for personal judgement. People are unlikely to be popular in the marching band if they want to play at their own tempo. By contrast, composing (inventing) offers the great-est scope for choosing not only *how* but *what* to play or sing and in which temporal order. Since composing gives more decision-making to the participant it allows more scope for cultural choice. Composing is thus an educational necessity, not some optional activity when time permits. It gives students an opportunity to bring their own ideas to the micro-culture of the classroom, infusing formal education with music from 'out there'. Teachers then become aware not only of the musical pathways of students but also to some extent of their social and personal worlds.

Both composing and performance taken as single educational activities limit us to what we can ourselves play or sing. If formal music education is to contribute to ongo-ing, 'situated' musical discourse, it should offer more than this. Also in the world outside of classrooms is the 'conversation' of musical thinking from other times and places, recorded and in live performance. Access to this literature must also be part of the experience of students in formal education. Composing, performing *and* audience-listening each have their part to play. In this way individual differences of students can be respected – the second principle. For we all ultimately find our own unique ways through the varieties of musical discourse.

Third principle: fluency first and last

If music is a form of discourse then it is in some ways analogous to, though not iden-tical with, language. The acquisition of language seems to involve several years or more of mainly aural and oral engagement with other 'languagers'. We have to look for the equivalent, of engagement with other 'musicers', long before any written text or other analysis of what is essentially intuitively known. This is clearly the position of people such as Orff, Jacques-Dalcroze and Suzuki and I think also to some extent of Kodály, for whom a rich background of singing 'by ear' is assumed *before* children begin to read music in the *Choral Method*. Unlike Kodály, however, I do not think that literacy is the ultimate aim of music education, it is simply a means to an end when we are working with *some* music. It is very often unnecessary. In any event (again on an analogy with language) the most effective procedural sequence is often: listen, articulate, then read and write. We might consider how this would affect the first few piano lessons, classroom instrumental work, choral or band rehearsals.

Musicians from outside western classical traditions are well aware of this third principle, that musical fluency takes precedence over musical literacy. It is precisely fluency, the aural ability to image music coupled with the skill of handling an instrument (or the voice), that characterises jazz, Indian music, rock music, music for steel-pans, a great deal of computer-assisted music and folk music anywhere in the world. Notation of any kind has limited or no virtue for performers of Korean *sanjo*, or Texas-Mexican *conjunto* accordion music, or *salsa*, or Brazilian *capoeira*. These musicians have much to teach about the virtues of playing 'by ear' and of the possibilities of extended musical memory and collective improvisation.

> I can teach you about three drum phrases and you can learn how to play them very well. But having mastered these phrases, you will develop an interest in drumming so that everywhere you go and wherever you hear someone drumming, you will approach him (or her). You will then learn other drum patterns in addition to those I have taught you. At any time I in particular hear *Agbadza* being played anywhere, I go there to listen to other drum phrases to add to those that I already know. So my experience deepens.
>
> (The Ghanaian master drummer, Godwin Agbeli, speaking with Robert Kwami about musical fluency in aural traditions (Kwami 1989: 104))[1]

Playing by ear has many facets. Philip Priest has identified at least nine. They include playing (or singing) a piece learned from notation from memory, specifically copying the playing of another performance, more generally imitating a style of playing heard some time before, improvising a variation on remembered music, inventing within a clear assimilated framework – such as a chord sequence – and free invention where the player (or singer) has maximum scope for choice and decision-making (Priest 1989). Students in any kind of formal music education should surely be able to engage in at least some of these very natural musical strategies.

Taken together, the three principles help to keep music teaching on track, to keep it 'musical'. Care for music as discourse, care for the musical discourse of students and an emphasis on fluency are likely to be more effective across a range of teaching settings than the detail of curriculum documentation. They help us think about the *quality* of music education, about the *how* rather than the *what*.

Principles in practice: four illustrations

1 The Tower Hamlets project

At this point I want to offer further examples of music education in practice that illustrate these three principles at work. The first is based on an account of the internationally recognised work of Sheila Nelson and her team who were working in several East London primary schools during the late 1980s. We were able to study and evaluate this scheme, the Tower Hamlets string-teaching project, in a sustained way (Swanwick and Jarvis 1990: 9). The main stated aim of the project was to have children learn instruments in a socially engaging way that develops technical *and* musical aspects of playing while respecting the personal development of each child. In other words, there was concern for the first two principles.

During seven weeks towards the end of 1989, over 120 hours of teaching were observed in thirteen schools along with other sessions at a Saturday Music Centre. Initial earlier visits allowed us to pilot and modify an observation schedule based on the CLASP model of musical activities (Swanwick 1979). In this model five music classroom activities are identified. These are *Composing, Literature Studies* (handling information *about* music), *Audience Listening or 'audition'* (to other pupils, to the teacher or a recording), *Skill Acquisition* and *Performance*. These categories formed a basis for observation and analysis of the music sessions. We decided to event-sample what we were seeing, keeping a systematic account of the different activities that constituted each session. These sessions were either whole class lessons for around twenty-five students or for smaller back-up groups for more technical work.

The resulting data gave an impression of the systematic development of technical and aural skills – control of sound materials. This was always closely related to a strong sense of expressive and shaped musical performance, to expression and structural relationships. That is to say, most of the observed events fell into the categories either of *Skill Acquisition* or musical *Performance*.

Composing – usually as some form of improvisation – occurred frequently and regularly enough for children to regard it as a natural part of instrumental playing. For example, children were often invited to improvise an answering phrase to one played by the teacher and the invention of rhythm patterns was often part of the musicianship lessons, usually playfully or in the spirit of a game.

Literature studies – giving information *about* music, such as definitions of musical terms and signs and notational devices such as key, clef, stave and dynamics – always occurred in the context of a practical activity.

Audience-listening was not a priority in the main group sessions, although we did hear three teachers performing a trio to a class. Children were able to listen to themselves and each other more carefully in so-called back-up lessons, smaller classes, usually of between four and eight. In these sessions there would be demonstration of a new piece by a teacher, occasional performance by one pupil, or a small group of pupils to the rest of the class and encouragement of more critical and analytical listening by sharing a performance of a piece by playing a line each.

Skill acquisition – the principle of fluency first was very evident as a feature of the programme strongly influenced by both Roland and Suzuki. Physical or manipulative control was developed well ahead of notational skills. Bowing was rehearsed ahead of left-hand technique and made it possible to have very rhythmic playing from the start, while freedom and flexibility were encouraged by lifted bow strokes and tremolo. Left-hand technique was based on a naturally balanced position of the violin and a hand shape built from exercises to develop fluency, such as tapping on the table of the violin in high positions. The foundations of position change and *vibrato* are laid early on by developing mobility. Rhythmic confidence was encouraged by clapping and chanting words and by various games, often involving movement. Extensive use of singing and sol-fa helped develop notational skills and pitch discrimination.

Performance – making music together – was the essential focus of the scheme and the presence of good pianists brought even the earliest technical exercises and open-string tunes to musical life, giving expressive character and structure to the simplest of materials.

In most of these classes the musical outcomes were obvious. Children were acquiring confidence and competence with instruments, they were singing and playing, listening carefully, working together and valuing music-making. They were gaining access and contributing to the 'conversation' we call music. There was obvious care for music as a meaningful form of discourse – the first principle. As to the second principle, with such a structured and intensive teaching scheme it may be thought that the musical discourse of students might become subjugated to the methods and materials of the programme. In actuality many of the sessions were lively and interactive and the students were involved in making their own decisions, especially when contributing musical ideas as improvisers. Bear in mind also that these students were all in primary schools: the oldest was eleven. Recent research confirms many previous findings, obvious enough to most teachers, that the musical value systems of younger children tend not to be so strongly developed as those of teenagers (Papapanayiotou 1998). There is therefore greater acceptance among younger students of a wider range of musical idioms, including those encountered in schools and featured in instructional material. For them the issue of what kind of music is brought to the classroom is not so crucial as with teenagers and beyond. Even so, in this case the project material was varied and culturally rich.

The overall impression of one of the project 'cello teachers, Virginia Bennett, strongly coincided with ours. For her, the aim of music education was very clear and it was substantially embodied in the Tower Hamlets scheme. As she said:

> Music's purpose is not simply to make products for society. It is a valid life experience in its own right, which we should make understandable and enjoyable. It is an experience of the present. These children are living today, not learning to live for tomorrow. We must help every child experience music *now*.
>
> (Swanwick and Jarvis 1990: 40)

2 The master drummer

During his conversation with John Chernoff, the Ghanaian drummer Ibrahim Abdulai reflects upon the process of improvisation (Chernoff 1979: 109–10). Although this vignette may not be considered to be teaching in any formal sense, I would suggest that his attitude is essentially that of the teacher who is teaching music musically. He cares for music as discourse, he respects the discourse of other musicians and dancers and, of course, for him musical fluency is paramount. Within the discourse of music, notice how Ibrahim Abdulai is concerned that the listening dancers first orientate themselves to certain 'norms' of drumming patterns. He is aware of the second level of metaphor where familiar musical gestures are transformed into new relationships. An extended quotation seems in order.

If you find a style and you like it, you can continue beating it for some time so that people can hear it well before you bring some changes. You can't just start at this moment and then change to another style again. It's not good. You have to play for some few minutes, and you can compare the styles and the sound of the dance; you can be thinking, 'I want to bring this style inside. Will it be nice for this dance?' By then you can rely on the topic of the drum and pick a style which fits and put it inside. But to bring on the new style by heart [*i.e., on impulse*] is not good. You will spoil the dance. You have to follow my steps and play with respect.

'Play with respect?' I asked.

Yes. That is how I drum. I am playing with respect. I don't play roughly; I pay attention to what I play. Sometimes when you know something too much, you can do it in a rough way and add something unnecessary inside. I don't do that. If you are beating a drum, you shouldn't beat by heart. You can change styles any time or you can just continue beating a particular style if you want it. It is according to the dance.

We notice the 'teacher' at work here. He wants people to 'hear it well' before making changes to the rhythm. Then he can lead them on into other musical ideas, new relationships. He also is alert to the first principle, he respects the discourse of music and cares about what he does. 'I pay attention to what I play.' This is interwoven with the second principle, care for the 'students'. He is really concerned for the effect of his drumming on those who listen and dance.

As he is drumming, sometimes people are also dancing. He watches their feet and how they take their feet for the dance. He watches the movement of the body and the feet, and as the dancer takes his steps in the dance, he will drum according to it.

He plays 'with respect' for music and for those who hear it. He plays while anticipating that those who engage with his drumming may relate to it and find what Chernoff calls power in a personal form (Chernoff 1979: 169). He plays with an awareness of the metaphorical richness of music.

3 Music in a Scottish school

A student teacher is completing her final year on teaching practice in a Scottish school. She is working with a small class of 'Higher' students. They are 16–17 years old and will soon be taking an examination the results of which will help determine their access to university courses.

The prescribed topic is 'fugue', a possible recipe for boredom. She prepares the students for an encounter with the C minor fugue of Bach's *48 Preludes and Fugues, Book One*. She briefly explains the organising principle of the entries of different 'voices' and plays on the piano in a fully characterised way the first three entries of the subject, the ongoing countersubject and the sequential episodes. At every stage the students are involved in recognising and using the terminology for what she calls the 'features' of this piece. Her enthusiasm for this music is evident. She really cares for this particular fugue and she cares that each individual student finds his or her way into it. The first principle is fully evident.

As to the second principle, there is of course little opportunity here for the students to bring their own musical discourse into the arena. But they may do so in the next session, when they will be 'inventing' their own music. By then they will also have noticed the dancing quality and the fugal texture of the third movement of Bach's second *Brandenburg Concerto* and also the teasing delay of the entry of the third 'voice', the violin. They will have been invited to make the second metaphorical move: to hear 'tunes' in new relationships. And they will be able to use this device of delaying an expected event in their own compositions.

In a session of this kind there is obviously no opportunity to develop musical fluency, but we all go away with a strong aural impression of the music in our minds, with some understanding of the compositional processes and most of all with a sense of value and commitment, caught partly from the teacher and also from the opportunity to hear the music as *music* without any intrusive simultaneous spoken commentary.

4 Teaching in Brazil

The fourth of these illustrative accounts is once again somewhat personal. I should emphasise that I am here describing a series of related educational activities in order to illuminate the three principles in action. The specific material or approach is not being advocated for use by others. It is not a 'method'. Seventy-five students in Porto Alegre, southern Brazil, made me extremely welcome during September 1997 and I am very grateful to them. They engaged so enthusiastically and musically throughout a memorable week-long course and they all feature in this account.

The first activity in this project is most definitely teacher-directed. In the terminology of the sociologist Basil Bernstein, I have strongly framed the activity by the choice of teaching sequence. There is also strong classification in that I have not only chosen the

Approximate scoring

A = High indefinite pitch (triangles, bells, rattles, etc.)

B = Low indefinite pitch instruments

C = Metal/ wooden bars and flutes/ recorders

D = Guitars and other string instruments plucking single notes

In each instrumental line there should be at least one instrument able to ring on at this sign ⌒

Note: The length of each measure is up to the conductor. Be sure to emphasise differences between loud and soft (f and p) and between the short, stopped sounds and those left to ring on. Try different speeds. The interpretation can be quite dramatic if you wish or it can be more relaxed if taken at a slower speed with less extreme dynamics.

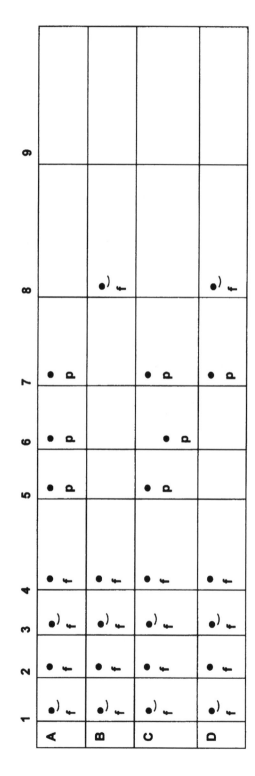

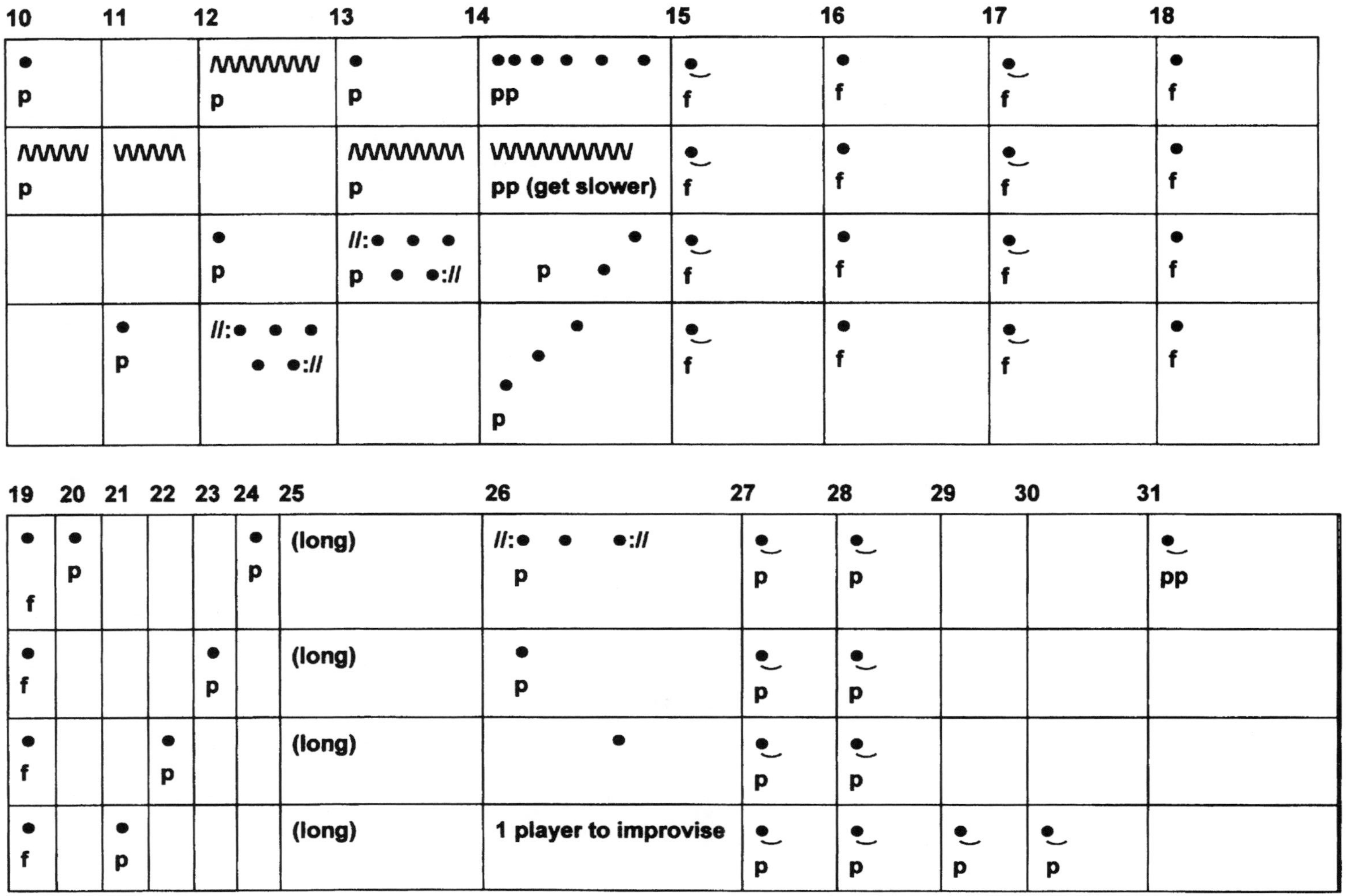

Music example 6 'Coming to understand'

musical content but have actually – for better or worse – composed it. This composition is neither ground-breaking in style nor one of the most original and significant works ever produced. However, it is a small contribution to the world of musical discourse and it played a positive part in the course as well as serving reasonably well to highlight the principles now under discussion.

a   In a concern for musical fluency and before getting us all glued to the notation, I have to make sure that the large group of students (all music teachers in some capacity) can produce the kind of sounds that are basic in this piece. Can they at a signal play together softly or loudly a single short sound? This means that on those instruments tending to resonate (triangles, cymbals, etc) the sounds have not only to be started but also stopped. These are fundamental techniques to be acquired by the players. Listening carefully is imperative.

b   Looking now for the first time at the notation, the signs for loud and soft, held over and stopped (damped) notes are identified and the first nine measures are played. Counting beats is not an option since each measure is a different length, judgements depending on the director. The ninth measure is a significant silence. Absolute precision is required from everybody and the passage is rehearsed until the players are fluent and are, once again, free from the notation: fluency first and fluency last. This passage could now be experienced as a paragraph, as a complete musical thought.

c   Most important, in transforming 'tones' into 'tunes' the sounds are heard and played in groups, phrases, gestures. At the start a bunch of sounds – many of them ringing on – prepare the way for the second, which seems more forceful because it is stopped short. The effect of this is that measures 1 and 2 become a single *gesture*. The gesture is repeated in measures 3 and 4. At this point we made the gesture even more emphatic in character, as repetitions often are. I cannot pretend that this simple idea and its repetition is novel. The opening of Beethoven's *Coriolanus Overture* comes to mind, though we were certainly not going to get involved with that.

d   Moving further into the piece, we then had to make sure that the new notational sign for continually activated sound that appears at measure 10 could be managed by all the players. We could then transform this particular 'tone' into the 'tune' that is passed from part to part between measures 10 and 14, a shimmering gesture gently interspersed with pin-point sounds.

e   The effect of the reprise at measures 15 to 18 has now to be decided. What is the relationship of this whole set of gestures to its first appearance? Should it have the same weight and spacing as before or be more or less emphatic? One way or other this decision will influence the winding down process towards the end. Has this actually begun at bar 15? If so, then the movement towards closure will probably be gradual. Or is this the last jagged outcrop of sound before a very steep descent? We were now deeply engaged with the first principle – care for music as discourse – and involved in the second strand of metaphor, the level of dynamic musical form.

f   Now two or three volunteer musical directors take over and are able to choose different speeds and alter the relative length of each measure. These are decisions which affect considerably the expressive potential. A faster speed drives the whole thing on so that a sense of urgency prevails, especially in measures 19 to 24. A slower speed brings about a more monumental and craggy feeling.

g   During the next few days and interwoven with many quite different activities, several small groups made their own interpretation of this score, one of them for voices only. They also became composers and invented short pieces using similar notation for the others to interpret and perform. In this way the second principle, that of student autonomy, came into play. Indeed, to some small extent this was so in measure 26, when one improvising player on the fourth instrumental line took off on guitar and we gave him plenty of time for what turned into a dance-like episode.

Because of the obvious constraints of working to this kind of score, even this last activity would not really be sufficient by itself to secure the second principle. However, we need to see this project in context. Among other activities were more open musical encounters involving response to words, aurally arranging a song and dramatising music. These openings released a wide range of musical styles, including atonal pieces, vocal jazz and samba. Even so, in spite of the limitations imposed by the graphic score, all three principles were kept in mind and guided the teaching: care for music as discourse, care for the discourse of students and musical fluency before music reading. Within the first principle the first two of the three metaphorical shifts were also evident. We went quite quickly from 'tones' to 'tunes' and began to see 'tunes' forming relationships with each other, giving the work its form, a 'life of its own'.

As to transforming these symbolic structures into significant new personal experience, who can tell? For some of us this may have been so. I do remember that during the same week the students worked in groups responding to a range of expressive ideas and linked these together into a larger form, an activity described elsewhere (Swanwick 1994: 123 ff). Among other ideas, they used musical devices picked up during this session with the graphic score. On encountering similar gestures presented powerfully within the dynamic structure of a recorded musical performance there were tearful eyes. We agreed just then that there was no more to be said and closed the session early. This, the third metaphorical shift into personal meaning, 'meaning for', cannot be predicted and is not always easily observed. When it does occur it displaces all alternative claims as to why music is valuable. The value lies in the revelation of pattern and form in our lives, however small or large this may happen to be. As we saw with Terence McLaughlin in the first chapter, we may 'find ourselves experiencing a synthesis or fusing of many events, many memories'. The Australian poet James McAuley put it this way:

Life holds its shape in the modes of dance and music,
The hands of craftsmen trace its patternings.
(McAuley 1965: 137)

Implicit in teaching music musically is a strong sense of life holding its shape or even *finding* its shape. This is why the first of the three principles is so crucial, that we care for music as discourse and proceed on the basis that it can make a difference to the way we live and how we reflect upon our living. The other two principles, concern for the discourse of students and promoting musical fluency, flow from this. These principles seem to me to be fundamental and can inform the work of any teacher in any setting using any chosen 'method', no matter how tightly or loosely organised. For what ultimately matters is the *quality* of musical experience in the 'here and now', the possibility that students may find their way into realms of metaphor that for them extend and populate the 'space between'.

The young man lives in a *favela* in Salvador, Brazil, in the *Candeal* area. An ambitious local scheme, '*Pracatum*', aims to facilitate the music-making and general education of young people and this has made it possible for him to organise a large group of teenage boys to play music together on indigenous instruments – drums, bells and rattles. He is a born leader and a naturally gifted teacher. These boys seem able to follow him in his musical imagination, no matter how demanding this becomes. He has developed a fluid and highly articulated system of hand-signals through which different rhythms and changes in combinations of instruments can be indicated. As they stand in lines the boys watch him and respond with a range of tightly controlled but highly expressive musical ideas. He mixes these gestures into forms in which ideas are replaced but may reappear and where sudden silences often serve to frame outbursts of incredible rhythmic energy. Sometimes during the music he walks between the teenagers gently showing how and what to play. Very rarely he rebukes them for not really watching, for not really listening. For the most part his musical direction is so graphically explicit that – like the best symphonic conductors – it all seems to happen by 'sleight of hand'. Very few words are spoken and no one attempts to talk while music is being made.

The first principle is strongly evident. The young man has tremendous care for music as discourse, as meaningful conversation. There is also some care for the discourse of members of the band. Many of the patterns that they play are drawn from the vernacular world of the *favela*, of street music. But these ideas are taken up into musical forms which open up avenues of significant new experience for all of us. This is evident in the intense concentration and strong sense of value which pervades the entire activity. His dream for the future, he tells me afterwards, is to make a perfect and extended musical work.

Later on he teaches me some basic patterns and, when I have them under control, he and a friend elaborate on them with other ideas on nearby instruments. Musical fluency is what matters here. This music will never be constrained by the analytical schemes of written notation. But it *is* music and it shares with other music the potential of metaphor: 'tones' become 'tunes', these expressive gestures are interrelated in new forms and these forms can have the power to reach into our histories, there to bring about transformations of the ways we construe the 'life of feeling' in ourselves and others. It may not be entirely a coincidence that this *favela* is much safer than so many are, both to live in and to visit.

How, though, can we ever know where students are as they work within this matrix of metaphorical layers? Is it possible, not only to teach musically, but also to assess the work of students musically? It is not only possible but essential. For there can be no teaching in any real sense of that word without sensitive and responsive assessment. It is perhaps unfortunate that student assessment has become a political issue linked to educational accountability. The growing number of tools for formal assessment are not often crafted musically and do not always reflect a really musical perspective. In the next chapter I hope to show how we can improve on this.

Note

1 Agbadza is a popular Ghanaian dance of the Anlo Ewe people of south-eastern Ghana. It is performed at social occasions of various sorts – at funerals, durbars, and so on. Its instrumentation is a double clapperless bell, enmeshed rattle, and three drums – kagan (small), kidi (medium) and sogo (master).

Chapter 4

The why and how of musical assessment

I have argued that music is a symbolic activity, an important form of human discourse. Three strands of metaphor are fundamental to this process and these give rise to four layers of musical functioning. From this perspective on the nature and value of music, it has been possible to identify three fairly strong principles for music education. In this chapter I want to turn to another practical application of this theory: the musical assessment of students' work. For genuinely musical assessment is a key to effective education.

The story goes that someone inherited a large sum of money and wanted to invest it wisely. A friend advised her to take up the collection of jade, to become a connoisseur. He recommended ten classes on jade collection with the celebrated Dr Chan. So the novice jade-collector paid up for ten lessons in advance. After several weeks she met her friend again. 'Fine advice you gave me,' she said. 'I've wasted a lot of money. I went for all of the ten lessons. Each time Dr Chan gave me a piece of green stone and sent me away into a room to sit and look at it. Nothing happened for an hour. I just sat there. Then Chan came back in. She took the stone away and showed me out. This happened every time. That's not proper teaching. And I'll tell you something else. The last one she showed me was a *fake*!'

Many of our most significant learning experiences may be tacit, unspeakable, incommunicable, and apparently out of reach of assessment, certainly of formal testing and examinations. But teachers usually have to respond more overtly to what students do.

Unfortunately we cannot always proceed with the quiet confidence of Dr Chan, certainly not when there are obligations to be explicit, to tell other people what we think we know. In any case it seems only fair to be honest about how we make judgements of the musical activity of others. For just as there are ways of teaching musically – or not, so there are ways of assessing musically – or not.

Musical activity is very widely assessed in all kinds of ways, including during graded instrumental and vocal examinations, auditions, festivals and competitions. Musical performances and compositions are subject to daily public review in the newspapers, and charts of recording sales plot the ups and downs of pieces and performers. And of course, musicians can be hired or fired on an assessment of the way they perform. In educational settings it is particularly necessary to understand what we are about. For existing practices can certainly be improved and it may be possible to develop more sensitive and effective ways of assessing musical achievement.

The functions of assessment

We assess the speed of traffic when we cross the road; in conversation we assess when the right moment may have arrived to say what we really think; when applying for a job we assess our chances; when out walking we assess how muddy the path in front might be and whether it really is a good idea to take it. When going downhill on skis . . .

Figure 3 Downhill all the way!

Assessment makes it possible for us to live – it guides all our actions. Assessing in everyday situations is often informal, intuitive. There is usually no standard procedure to follow, no need to carry out any detailed analysis, no requirement to submit a written report. Indeed, when crossing the road, if we were to stop to analyse mathematically the angles of approach and quantify the exact speed of traffic, we would be at serious risk. We see this informality at work in our daily judgements about music. For example, we might turn on the car radio and find that it emits a performance of a type of music that at that time we just do not want to hear. Either we switch off or we change the channel. We filter the music out, our response is the simple act of *rejection*. In these circumstances we may be hearing music as *sign* or *signal*, rather than *symbol*.

Filtering has a more positive side, that of *selection*. We may go out of our way to be near a radio or make a tape recording when something we really want to listen to is being broadcast. Or we may keep on the lookout for the latest disc of particular performers or performances. Here we are actively filtering *in*. Every time we choose to listen to music we make one of these 'filtering in' assessments. And the whole process is usually totally intuitive and unspoken. We do not have to justify our preferences to anyone, fill in comment forms or give a mark out of ten. We simply make up our minds and get on with it.

If assessment is intuitively so much a part of daily life, why is it that assessment in education and especially in the arts appears to be problematic? It is when we find ourselves moving away from informal assessment that things start to get tricky. For assessment ranges from making instantaneous choices in our daily life to the relative formality of analytical reporting. I can sympathise with anyone who fears getting caught up in the machinery of assessment or has worries that the magic of music will suffer through being processed by the clanking apparatus of marks and grades. There is, though, more to it than that.

Filtering		Teaching		Examining	
Rejecting	Selecting	Interacting	Comparing	Testing	Reporting

Informal ———————————————————————————————— Formal

Figure 4 The functions of assessment

Moving across into the centre of Figure 4, we notice that in educational transactions teachers do far more than simply reject and select. They *interact* with what students say and do. And this type of assessment can still be relatively informal.

> The teacher points out and discusses the relationship between aspects of the music, querying anomalies, drawing attention to special strengths, and suggesting extra possibilities. He or she discusses what skills are needed for the task in hand, to what extent they have been successfully deployed, how they might be perfected, what further skills might more fully realise the music, and how these might best be acquired.
>
> The teacher tries to get the pupils to bring fully into play their own listening and self-criticism, so that the process becomes an interaction between self-assessment and teacher-assessment.
>
> This *is* assessment in the most educationally important sense of the word.
>
> (Loane 1982: 242)

Teachers also make *comparisons*. These comparisons might be intra-personal, that is to say, between what a particular student happens to be doing just now and what was happening with the same student last week or perhaps last year. In what particular ways is this composition, this performance or this talk about music different from or the same as before? Comparisons may also be *inter-personal*, made between different students. The level of informality diminishes when comparisons begin to be made with the work of *other* students. We may have to search for a meaningful shared vocabulary or to find and declare criteria that make sense to everyone. Even more formal are attempts at making comparisons with some kind of *norm*, perhaps with what students at a certain age or at a particular stage of a course might usually be expected to achieve. It is at the point of comparison that we begin to become aware of a need for reliable touchstones, for explicit standards, for a shared language of musical criticism.

Brian Loane paints a very good picture of formative interaction. However, this by itself, though absolutely essential, is not always sufficient. Teachers inevitably find themselves drawn into making assessments of a more formal kind, for example, when needing to justify decisions to other people, to heads of institutions, to parents, to prospective employers. Above all, though, they are accountable to their students. We do not get very far without having to answer important questions: 'Why do you say that?' 'What is wrong with it?' 'What do you mean?' Much more formality is apparent when we are obliged to report comparisons to people beyond the immediate transaction, perhaps in conversation with or writing notes to parents, or when producing a comment for a school report. Unlike the richer conversations that characterise teaching, the ultimately formal assessment statement is likely to be cryptic: perhaps a brief statement, a number, a grade or a degree classification. It is here that judgements can be most hotly disputed. For personal feelings, public prestige, jobs and reputations may be at stake.

So it is, then, that along the continuum of assessment, which ranges from informal and often instantaneous response to the formalised rigours of reports, tests and examinations, teachers find themselves playing several different roles. Assessing takes place in different ways and for various purposes. My concern here is mainly with the practicalities of formal assessment. For having a clearer understanding of how formally to assess music *musically* can also help in the daily informal processes of interacting and comparing.

The dimensions of musical assessment

Teachers have to be sensitive and articulate critics. The first requirement of a music critic is to acknowledge the complexity of musical experience. Such a rich activity cannot be reduced to a single dimension, say, that of instrumental or vocal 'technique'. There are the other commonly recognised elements, including what is sometimes vaguely called 'musicality' or 'musicianship'. Yet it seems to defy the holistic nature of any artistic activity to identify several different dimensions and try to give separate marks for each. In assessing a composition or improvisation, for example, I have seen schemes which require marks for melody, harmony and texture which are then added up to get a single figure. When conflating several different observations we lose a lot of important information on the way. For instance, in competitive ice skating one performer might be given six out of ten for technique and nine for artistry, while another contender gets nine for technique and only six for artistry. The sum of each set of marks happens to be the same – fifteen – but our impression of the actual performances will be quite different. The common fudge of adding a category called 'overall' only makes things worse.

In any case, we ought to resist falling back on the poor levels of meaning embodied in numerical marks and we ought to beware of the false impression of exact quantification that numbers can give. Nor can we assume that more of something (say greater instrumental agility) necessarily means better (performance). For instance, we might be tempted to think that playing a relatively uncomplicated lyrical piece is of less musical value than throwing off a virtuoso delivery. Surely the person playing the 'easy' piece ought not to get such high marks as the other? This way of thinking is really not satisfactory and may make too much of virtuosity. It could lure performers into water that is technically too deep for the good of their musical development.

There is a further problem. How can we equate the differing technical demands of say, a piano performance of a Chopin mazurka, a Scott Joplin rag and a Bach fugue? While Bach requires clear and balanced part-playing with matching articulation for each appearance of the same material, both Chopin and Joplin need an accurately placed left hand and careful colouring of the chords in the inside parts that does not detract from the elaborate flow of melody above. It might be hard to say which piece is the most demanding to play; there are different difficulties. Yet in spite of obvious differences we can find some things in common between a musician playing one piece and someone else playing another; in the same way that it is possible to say of a well-known tennis player, an Olympic high-jumper and an international footballer that they are all fine athletes. We do this by applying general criteria that define what it means to be athletic. In the same way, there are qualities that we recognise as musical wherever they appear. Can we identify these qualities? If we can then we are on the way towards declaring our criteria for musical assessment, towards putting our cards on the table. The task is challenging. What are we looking for?

I suggest that we cannot go so very far adrift if we stay close to the idea of music as metaphor and concentrate on the visible external layers on either side of each metaphorical transformation. The psychological leaps are hidden from view but the

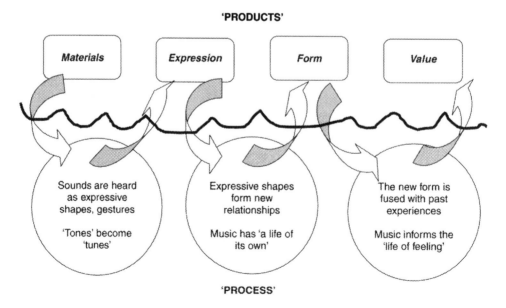

Figure 5 Process and product in metaphorical change

places of arrival can be observed in what we do and say. These observable layers have already been identified as *Materials, Expression, Form* and *Value*. It may be helpful once again to be reminded of the relationship between these and their metaphorical basis.

Remember that the upper lozenge shapes are, so to speak, the layers above the waterline. Perhaps it is because of the hidden metaphorical processes that people sometimes feel that assessment in music and the other arts is impossible or inappropriate. But there are the visible 'products' of the four layers wherein lies evidence as to the level of our involvement when we make music or listen to the music of others. We can see these four layers quite clearly if we step back from the clutter of those assessment schemes we happen to know and look at the fundamental processes of assessment more imaginatively.

Salieri takes his first look at the score of Mozart's Wind Serenade in B Flat
On the page it looked nothing; the beginning simple, almost comic, just a pulse – bassoons, basset-horns – like a rusty squeezebox. And then, suddenly – high above it – an oboe, a single note hanging there, unwavering, until a clarinet took it over, sweetening it into a phrase of such delight. This was no performing monkey. This was a music I had never heard, filled with such longing, such unforgettable longing. It seemed to me that I was hearing the voice of God.
(From the play and film *Amadeus*, by Peter Shaffer.)

Why is this often quoted piece of fiction so striking? I suggest because it is an almost archetypal response to music, a poetic description hinting at the rich interweaving of the various layers of musical understanding. At the outset, Salieri has an impression mainly of particular sonorities from which he can instantly 'place' the music as simple, comic – the kind of thing he has heard so many times before. He can, of course, imagine the instrumental texture and its mundane 'squeezebox' effect. Many of his contemporaries would hear it as aural wallpaper. That would be its main social function. But Salieri knows that music is a form of discourse and goes further into it, becoming aware of the high oboe note which soon evolves into a phrase which moves to the clarinet. This transforms his first impression. A metaphorical shift occurs and a bunch of commonplace instrumental sounds are heard sequenced into expressive gestures.

The score is snatched away from Salieri before he can say more about his structural explorations of this movement but he is left with such a feeling of its value, 'the voice of God', that his whole life is changed. Here then – in Salieri's (or Shaffer's!) musical assessment – are the three metaphorical shifts and the four resulting layers: sound materials transform into expressive gestures, these shapes are woven into new forms and these structures 'in-form' his world of values.

Children make musical judgements in similar ways (Hentschke 1993). An 8-year-old immediately latched on to the kind of sounds and was able to 'place' the introduction to Phil Collins singing 'That's Just the Way It Is'. She also immediately filtered the music and categorised it into a type, not 'simple, almost comic', but 'a pop star would sing this'. And she too noticed the sound materials, the instrumentation – 'it was a drum'.

A 10-year-old goes further than this, telling us that the music had 'wooden instruments at the beginning and strings, had a drum beat, the wooden instruments at the beginning had a pattern and later it went faster, relaxing after the percussion instruments'. She notices the expressive effect of patterns and the changes in speed, which she is able to characterise expressively as 'relaxing'. She also tells us more about instrumentation, though it is in fact a keyboard simulation rather than strings that we hear.

By the age of 13 or so, young people are likely to relate to expressive character even more strongly and to tell us more about their perception of form. Here is someone telling us that the beginning of this same recording

> makes you feel the music rather than listen to it, because it makes you take notice of what was actually played – very nice and very 'flowy'. The second part was very bouncy and then comes the flowy part. I like this type of music best, because you can feel it, and [it] makes you feel involved. It sounded like night, but when the drums come in it sounded like stones falling.

Here it seems taken for granted that drums are playing. The point is that they change the character of expressiveness from 'flowy' to 'stones falling' – an engagement that lies at the centre of our understanding of musical form. For musical form is about relationships, not only between larger architectural blocks but also more organically between gestures, patterns, phrases. These can be heard as repeated, transformed or contrasted, this can lead us on expectantly, sometimes surprising us – 'suddenly – an oboe, a single note hanging there', or, 'then comes the "flowy" part'.

We can also see in some of these responses a direct empathy with music. It 'makes you feel involved', or – more grandly – we are 'filled with such longing'. Reflecting on our own musical experiences, we know how our responses can grow into a strong sense of the value of music, a celebration of its human significance. If we are to attempt a proper assessment of musical understanding the issue of valuing really cannot be avoided. An involved commitment to music is a necessary requirement of the best composition and performance and is a frequent outcome of intense listening. In formal assessment we cannot ignore any of the layers.

Formal assessment and musical quality

Music curriculum guidelines for schools and their associated assessment assumptions and models multiplied rapidly during the 1990s. They illustrate very clearly the problems and possibilities of formal assessment. I shall concentrate here on those schemes I know best, although I believe that what I have to say applies to many others.

Those responsible for the respective National Curriculum documentation for music in both England and Wales seem to have assembled a model of assessment without any attempt to validate or check reliability (ACAC 1996; ACAC 1997; SCAA 1996a; SCAA 1996b). These materials raise misgivings about whether the procedures really assess musical work *musically* and whether the assessment results are consistent between assessors and over time. I have dealt with this elsewhere (Swanwick 1997). Just now I note only that in the Welsh National Curriculum the following expressions, while apparently suggesting assessment possibilities, really defy definition: 'increasingly complex', 'increasing attention to detail', 'subtle changes', 'increasingly demanding', 'increasing awareness', 'sophisticated techniques', 'refine', 'appropriate', 'challenging demands'. The English version also has a few doubtful candidates such as 'subtle changes' and 'appropriately'.

There is also an unfortunate attempt to illuminate the concept of progression with such phrases as 'more complex structures', 'more complex aspects of musical knowledge' and 'greater musicality' (SCAA 1996a). Such language is too imprecise and spuriously quantitative to form the basis of a viable assessment model. Furthermore, suggested criteria would give a curious result if applied, for instance, to many of Bach's single subject fugues. Though conceived for performance on a keyboard they stay within a vocal range and therefore do not 'make full use of the technical possibilities of instruments' (SCAA 1996a: 13). Nor is there a 'wide range of ideas', since these fugues often tend to have but one main subject and a single counter theme. Indeed a fugue such as the one in D sharp minor, Book One of the *48 Preludes and Fugues*, is concerned only with its subject. On this evidence and using contemporary assessment jargon, we would have to say either that Bach is only 'working towards' or is just 'achieving' the musical competence expected of an assumed typical 13-year-old.

Similar problems seem to occur also in the United States. The *National Standards for Arts Education* also sees attempts to formulate criteria for assessing the musical achievement of students (MENC 1994: 78–9). Here again there is a tendency to equate more with better. For example, a five-point scale is offered for levels of performance difficulty, from 'very easy', through 'moderately easy', to 'difficult'. 'Difficult' really seems to mean having *more* of things: more key signatures, more sharps and flats, more time signatures, more variety of rhythm patterns, more notes. Terms such as 'limited ranges' contrasted with 'expanded ranges' and 'various interpretative requirements' confirm the impression that musical progress is quantitative rather than qualitative. Indeed, I am reminded of a colleague in a school in which I taught who observed that a pupil was obviously an exceptionally gifted musician, since he played the school organ *faster* than anyone had ever played it before.

The problem of what to make of different levels of technical difficulty has often perplexed those attempting to formulate assessment procedures in music. This has been called variously 'complexity' (ACAC 1996), 'demand' (SCAA 1996a) and 'level of difficulty' (MENC 1994). 'Complexity' obviously relates to the kind of job in hand but it depends also on the response that particular individuals make. For example, an assignment might be to compose a 'simple' piece of music using only the notes of a pentatonic scale. An imaginative student might decide to employ these same notes as a canon in a composition, perhaps with accompanying pentatonic chord clusters. This would obviously be more complex, demanding or difficult in the sense that there would be more variables to control, in the same way that the added drone extended the performance requirements in the 'OAKE' song which was discussed in the previous chapter. However, the choice of resources here is the student's own and they will presumably lie within that person's sphere of technical control. This is important, as we shall see later on. Complexity may include the management and appraisal of simultaneous parts, harmonic, rhythmic and melodic elaboration and awareness of structural relationships within extended compositions or performances. But the *quality* of the composition cannot be evaluated in these terms. Complexity by itself is no virtue. Performing a wide range of complex music without evidence of understanding would definitely not count as a high level of achievement. And it is certainly possible to perform, compose and enjoy a high quality of musical experience without any great complexity.

One attempt to get around the issue of relative complexity is the use of what are sometimes called 'difficulty multipliers', where a student's marks are amplified when music that is thought to be more difficult is performed. This procedure seems at odds with the idea of musical quality. Of course we may want to see that students extend their technical range. But not in every piece! Sometimes it is the *musical* range that needs extension and the question then becomes not 'how many notes?' but 'how many layers?'. This is what I mean by *quality* in music-making and musical appraisal and it can be missing or present, no matter how simple or complex the technical materials happen to be. If we really want to get some idea of the technical range of the student, then we should take into account several performances or compositions produced over a period of time. After all, we do not always have to function on the edge of the virtuosic.

As we have already seen, in an attempt to pick up the idea of musical quality, nebulous terms get thrown into the assessment picture. But undefined words like 'subtle' and 'appropriate', offer very little by way of illumination. For example, the American 'Standards' criteria for performance define the terms 'expression' and 'expressive' as 'appropriate' dynamics and phrasing, or with 'appropriate' variations in dynamics and tempo (MENC 1994: 78). But what does 'appropriate' mean? We really have no idea since, in spite of a long preliminary discussion of why the arts are important to life and learning (pages 8 and 9), nowhere is there any consideration of the specific nature and communicative function of artistic expressiveness.

Furthermore, there are significant curiosities in the details of the standards for various grades. For example, students in Grades 5–8 are to arrange 'simple pieces for voices or instruments'. By Grades 9–12 the word simple is omitted and they are also to 'preserve or enhance the expressive effect of the music'. Is the implication, then, that students up to the age of 13 are not expected to be aware of and care for expressive character? A similar suggestion occurs in the activity called 'listening to, analysing, and describing music'. Describing 'expressive devices' is not required until Grades 9 to 12. Yet we know that young people by the age of 6 are more than able to produce and identify not only general mood or atmosphere in music but also specific musical gestures. And by the age of 10 or so, they are usually aware of structural transformations between and within musical gestures, sensitive to the organic processes of musical form (Swanwick and Tillman 1986).

After listening whilst following the score, a school student from Wales aged about 12–13 wrote her thoughts about Berio's *Sequenza Five*, the one for trombone solo.

The vowels were voiced to sound like the instrument. A plunger mute was used on some of the notes. This made the notes softer. It gave a good effect because it contrasted. It gave a sort of relaxing mood, though some of the notes were quite

abrupt. The voice saying the vowels gave a sort of humorous effect. I think the
whole piece was repeated again. It was louder and sometimes slower than before.
It was effective because you were relaxed the first time – you woke up the second
time. It gave a more busy feeling, almost as though there were more things going
on in the music. At the end 'Why?' gave an ending to the three lines. I liked it
because it was different, but I don't think I'd like to play it.

In this context, 'relaxing', 'humorous', 'abrupt' and 'busy' are mainly expressive character words. She draws our attention to relationships, to organic musical form, with
terms such as 'contrasted' and 'the whole piece repeated (but louder and slower)' and
her observation about the effect of the concluding 'Why?'. There even seems to be a
suggestion of valuing, though it is hard to be sure on this evidence alone.

One further brief example will suffice to show the difficulty that committees are
liable to get themselves into when trying to prescribe forms of student assessment without an underlying model of music understanding. During 1998 the Federation of
Music Services (FMS) and National Association of Music Educators (NAME) in the
United Kingdom produced a joint document, *A Common Approach*, intended to set up
a framework for an instrumental or vocal curriculum (FMS/NAME 1998). Although
the various programmes of study are headed 'Playing and singing with expression',
there is precious little in the detailed sets of learning objectives that fleshes out this
design. Over a large number of specific items (sixty-five) there are only two or three
objectives that clearly deviate from the purely technical, and all of these are to be
elicited in discussion about music rather than observed in performance or composing.
Even these two are but vague references to the mood and character of music. There is
nothing explicit concerning students' understanding of the essential internal relationships that constitute musical form.

Some of the confusion over formal assessment might have been avoided had the
dimension of musical understanding received explicit attention from the start. It would
then have been possible to develop a basis for teachers to assess the *quality* of pupils'
work, however simple or complex the music happens to be. There has been sustained
research in several countries which suggests that it is indeed helpful to think of musical understanding being revealed in the four layers we identified earlier and which have
been discussed in other publications (Swanwick 1979; Swanwick 1983; Swanwick
1988; Swanwick and Tillman 1986). These are the dimensions in which all musical
criticism and analysis is framed, areas in which philosophers of art, aestheticians and
psychologists have laboured for centuries. It seems then not unreasonable to have them
infiltrate our thinking on assessment:

Awareness and control of *sound materials*: shown in distinguishing between timbres, levels of loudness, duration or pitches, technical management of instruments or voices;

Awareness and control of *expressive character*: shown in atmosphere, musical gesture, the sense of movement implied in the shape of musical phrases;

Awareness and control of musical *form*: shown in relationships between expressive shapes, the ways in which musical gestures are repeated, transformed, contrasted or connected;

Awareness of the personal and cultural *value* of music: shown in autonomy, independent critical evaluation and sustained commitment to specific musical styles.

This model can be further articulated by recognising that each of these statements has two aspects, the first relating to the 'subjective' personal musical worlds of individuals and the second to the public worlds of musical practices and traditions – a distinction between intuitive and analytical modes of understanding which I have developed elsewhere (Swanwick 1994). These are the qualities that thread their way through the fabric of musical experience and they happen to be very robust in day-to-day use. Condensed to the briefest possible format and formulated as observable criteria they can be applied to composing, performing and also to audience-listening. It is important to remember that they are *cumulative*. The later statements take in and include all preceding layers.[1] The text in brackets relates to performing and composing.

General criteria for assessing the musical work of students

Materials

Level 1 recognises (*explores*) sonorities, for example, loudness levels, wide pitch differences, well-defined changes of tone colour and texture.

Level 2 identifies (*controls*) specific instrumental and vocal sounds – such as types of instrument, ensemble or tone colour.

Expression

> *Level 3*   (*communicates*) expressive character in music – atmosphere and ges-
> ture – or can interpret in words, visual images or movement.
> *Level 4*   analyses (*produces*) expressive effects by attention to timbre, pitch,
> duration, pace, loudness, texture and silence.

Form

> *Level 5*   perceives (*demonstrates*) structural relationships – what is unusual or
> unexpected, whether changes are gradual or sudden.
> *Level 6*   (*makes*) or can place music within a particular stylistic context and
> shows awareness of idiomatic devices and stylistic processes.

Value

> *Level 7*   reveals evidence of personal commitment through sustained engage-
> ment with particular pieces, performers or composers.
> *Level 8*   systematically develops (*new music processes*) critical and analytical
> ideas about music.

These general criteria serve assessment purposes quite well, though they need to be applied in specific musical contexts. Variations of the criteria have been rigorously tested in a variety of performing and composing settings and they have also been found helpful when assessing the responses of students as 'audience-listeners' (Hentschke 1993; Swanwick 1994). During 1997 one of our research students, Cecilia Cavalieri França, developed a version of these criteria in Portuguese for the most difficult area, that of audience-listening, an assessment mode where information from students is second-hand, usually in words rather than in music (Silva 1998). She gave randomised sets of the eight statements to twelve 'judges' – teacher musicians – who were asked independently of each other to sort them into a hierarchy. The predicted order was as follows.

Audience-Listening Criteria

> *Level 1* – The student recognises sound qualities and effects, perceives clear dif-
> ferences of loudness level, pitch, timbre, tone colour and texture. None of these is
> technically analysed and there is no account of expressive character or structural
> relationships.

Level 2 – The student perceives steady or fluctuating beats, identifies specific instrumental and vocal sounds, devices related to the treatment of musical material, such as *glissandi, ostinati,* trills; yet s/he does not relate these elements to the expressive character and structure of the piece.

Level 3 – The student describes the expressive character, the general atmosphere, mood or feeling qualities of a piece, maybe through non-musical associations and visual images. S/he relates changes in the handling of sound materials, especially speed and loudness, with changes of expressive level, but without drawing attention to structural relationships.

Level 4 – The student identifies commonplaces of metric organisation, sequences, repetitions, syncopation, drones, groupings, *ostinato*; s/he perceives conventional musical gestures and phrase shape and length.

Level 5 – The student perceives structural relationships, the ways in which musical gestures and phrases are repeated, transformed, contrasted, or connected. S/he identifies what is unusual or unexpected in a piece of music; perceives changes of character by reference to instrumental or vocal colour, pitch, speech, loudness, rhythm and phrase length, being able to discern the scale in which changes take place, whether they are gradual or sudden.

Level 6 – The student places music within a stylistic context and shows awareness of technical devices and structural procedures which characterise an idiom, such as distinctive harmonies and rhythmic inflections, specific instrumental or vocal sounds, decoration, transformation by variation, contrasting middle sections.

Level 7 – The student is aware of how sound materials are organised to produce a particular expressive character and stylistically coherent formal relationships. There are individual insights and independent critical appraisal. S/he reveals a feeling of valuing of music which may be evidenced by an account of personal involvement in a chosen area of music-making and/or a sustained engagement with particular works, composers or performers.

Level 8 – The person reveals a profound understanding of the value of music due to a developed sensitivity with sound materials, the ability to identify expression and comprehend musical form. There is a systematic commitment to music as a meaningful form of symbolic discourse.

In the hierarchical 'sort' of these statements there was considerable judge accordance. The agreed order also matches perfectly the predicted hierarchical order.[2] We can, then, feel reasonably confident about these criteria as an assessment instrument. They are reliable as an instrument of assessment and, as we shall see, can be very useful in evaluating teaching and learning in music.

Formal assessment is but a very small part of any classroom or studio transaction but it is important to get the process as right as we can, otherwise it can badly skew the educational enterprise and divert our focus from the centre to the periphery; from musical to unmusical criteria or towards summative concerns about range and complexity rather than the formative here-and-now of musical quality and integrity.

Student assessment and curriculum evaluation

There are many benefits from having a valid assessment model that is true to the rich layers of musical experience and, at the same time, is reasonably reliable. One of these possibilities is a richer way of evaluating teaching and learning, coming to understand more fully what is at issue in the classroom or studio. I shall give just one example of this, a recent study that really illuminates the relationship of the major music curriculum activities of composing, performing and audience-listening.

Any valid and reliable assessment model has to take account of two dimensions: what pupils are *doing* and what they are *learning*, curriculum activities on the one hand and educational outcomes on the other. Learning is the residue of experience. It is what remains with us when an activity is over, the skills and understanding we take away. Musical understanding lies in a different dimension from the musical activities through which this understanding may be revealed and developed – composing or improvising, performing the music of others, or responding in audience to music. This distinction is clear if we think for a moment of linguistic abilities. Converse for a time with a child of 4 or 5 and we are likely to hear a wide vocabulary with excursions into most grammatical forms, with appropriate prepositions, conjunctions, auxiliary verbs and so on. But examine the written language of the same child and, at such a young age, we are likely to find a much less advanced linguistic ability. The mode of articulation can reveal or conceal the level of understanding. I once supervised a PhD student from Korea who had systematically studied English at school, though almost entirely from books. Her conversation in English was understandably halting and difficult to follow and she often had to ask for something to be repeated before she understood what was said. And we also had to ask her for clarification of what she said. But her written essays – including her answers to previously unseen written, timed examination questions, without the benefit of any reference material – and her eventual PhD thesis all evinced ample evidence of a highly sophisticated use of English.

These are clear examples of the difference between activities and understanding and of how one activity can reveal more or less understanding than another. This is why it is usually unwise to rely only upon one type of evidence or just a single 'product' when trying to assess the work of students. Furthermore, it also follows that understanding may be developed more in one setting than another. For example, a gifted improviser who is asked to perform difficult music composed and notated by someone else may feel constrained and under pressure, unable to develop musical ideas freely. In this situation opportunities to function in a comprehensively musical way seem contracted rather than expanded, at least initially. Similarly, a fluent and sensitive performer may feel lost if asked to compose or improvise and may function at a level where musical understanding is neither revealed nor extended.

The activities of performing and composing may complement each other and insights gained in one domain might then inform the other. The performer who also composes is likely to be more aware of compositional processes and this understanding may illuminate subsequent performances. Many music educators certainly believe that composing, performing and audience-listening are activities that reinforce one another (Leonhard and House 1959; Mills 1991; Plummeridge 1991; Swanwick 1979).

> In an integrated and coherent music education in which children compose, perform and listen, the boundaries between musical processes disappear. When children compose, for instance, they cannot help but learn as performers and listeners.
>
> (Mills 1991)

Evidence for this has been produced by Dr Michael Stavrides who, working with teachers in Cyprus schools, found that students who listened to music produced more developed music in their own compositions (Stavrides 1995; Swanwick 1994). However, we ought not to assume that there will be a kind of 'symmetry' of musical understanding, that a pupil will have equal levels of understanding in the three domains of composing, performing and audience-listening. The examples given earlier of different levels of linguistic achievement and dependency on the specific context ought to make us cautious.

During 1997, Cecilia Cavalieri França worked with twenty Brazilian children in the city of Belo Horizonte (Silva 1998). These students were all between 11 and 13 years of age and were enrolled in music classes in one large private music school. In the general absence of music in Brazilian state schools, it is in the private sector where most music is taught. During this study, each child made recordings of three memorised piano performances (the piano being their main instrument), recorded three of their own compositions (produced 'aurally', without notation) and discussed and made written notes on three recorded pieces of music, all of which were heard three times. There were then nine 'products' from each child: three performances, three compositions and three in-audience responses. These musical products were assessed by four judges, all of them experienced teacher-musicians and they used 'best fit' statements which were based on the eight layers given above. This amounted to a total of 240 observations for each of the three activities. Figure 6 shows the distribution of these assessments. The results clearly reveal that while most of the children's work displayed matching levels of musical understanding for composing and audience-listening, their performances were less developed.

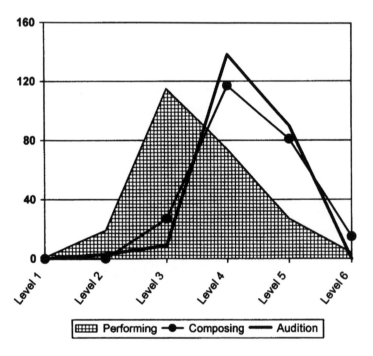

Figure 6 Musical activities and musical understanding

There is a striking symmetrical relationship between the assessments of audience-listening and composing, while performing attracts significantly lower levels of criterion descriptions.[3] It appears that the same children reveal less 'musicality' or musical *quality* when they play the music of other people than they do when they play their own pieces or discuss recorded music. What are we to make of this? Musical decision-making often seemed to go underground when they played their prepared piano pieces (from memory) while the activities of composing and audience-listening gave them opportunities to engage more richly with more layers of musical discourse. The performances were all played from memory although they were initially based on notated pieces. These pieces were practised over a longish period of time. One explanation is that after a time students cease to really listen to what they are doing, becoming satiated or even bored by repetition, as do members of bands and choirs when they over-rehearse a very limited repertory. Furthermore and importantly, the level of technical complexity is implicit in the choice of piece, whereas when composing these children often stepped back to a technical level within which they were able to make musical decisions, judgements about speed, about expressive shaping, about structural relationships. In audience-listening there are, of course, no technical problems.

Such comparisons across different activities only become possible with the aid of a half-way decent definition of musical understanding, a theory of musical mind. From such findings we can tease out several important implications. One of these is that it would be unwise to base a curriculum more or less exclusively on performing, whether through individual instrumental instruction or in ensembles. The argument and the evidence support the view that students should have access to a range of musical possibilities, including composing and audience-listening. Only then can we be sure that they are able to show and develop the full potential of their musical understanding.

It follows from all this that students should have the chance to produce and respond to music in all layers of musical discourse, whatever the activity. If students are not working at a level in which they can exercise truly musical judgements they are unlikely to be developing the quality of their musical thinking. This may sometimes mean drawing back from pushing into yet more technical work and instead making some space for expressive and structural musical decisions. In a comprehensive programme of music education, students should often find themselves in a position to make truly musical judgements, to transform and develop their own musical ideas and come to their own musical values. For individuals make their own metaphorical connections that enable them to move creatively between the layers of music. Students can then evaluate their own work and the work of others. Becoming an 'insider', being a part of the 'conversation', is what education is ultimately about. This alone makes meaningful assessment possible, including student 'self-assessment'. Curriculum activities and assessment processes that range across the various modes of musical encounter and venture through all four layers of musical discourse give students the possibility, freedom and responsibility for charting and following their own musical pathways.

Notes

1 The idea of cumulative layers is essentially Piagetian. Unfortunately, popular convention asserts quite wrongly that Piaget thought each stage somehow separate from the others. For example, Gardner asserts that for Piaget 'the child does not even have access to his earlier forms of understanding. Once he is out of a stage, it is as though the prior stage had never happened' (Gardner 1993: 26–7). This is certainly not my impression of Piaget. For example, when writing of the development of children through what he calls the successive structures – sensory-motor, symbolic, preconceptual, intuitive and rational – Piaget tells us plainly that 'it is essential to understand how each of these behaviours is continued in the one that follows, the direction being from a lower to a higher equilibrium. It is for this reason that in our view a static analysis of discontinuous, stratified levels is unacceptable' (Piaget 1951: 291).

2 A Kendall Coefficient of Concordance gives a W of 0.91 and a significance level of $p < 0.0001$. Moreover, a good indication of the nature of the consensus is the order of the sum of the ranks which matches perfectly the predicted hierarchical order.

3 A Friedman two-way ANOVA (analysis of variance) gives the following levels of probability: Composing and Audience listening – no significant difference, Performance compared with both Audience-listening and Composing – a significant difference of the order of $p < 0.001$.

Chapter 5

What of the future?

At the present time there is a growth of music educational 'outreach' expected from and initiated by arts agencies, orchestras, opera houses, community groups, music centres and many other agencies. This inevitably calls into question the relationship between schools or colleges and music-making elsewhere. And there is a great deal of this music. For example, in her study in the 1980s of music in a relatively new town in England (Milton Keynes, population around 100,000), Ruth Finnegan found music in ninety-two schools, but also elsewhere. There were eight brass bands, 100 choirs, 200 small bands – including pop, rock, folk, jazz – four classical orchestras and several chamber groups. There was music-making in many of the seventy churches. These activities were not located geographically or in clearly defined communities. Rather, there were musical 'pathways', roads through music chosen by each person (Finnegan 1989).

For now, then, let us put aside the technicalities of assessment and the ins-and-outs of curriculum design and look outside, beyond the confines of classroom and studio. In order to do this I shall describe in some detail a case study of one extensive outreach programme. This draws our attention to some possibilities for the future policy and organisation of what I have been calling 'formal' music education.

Resources beyond the school gate

Between 1994 and 1997 at the University of London Institute of Education, we carried out an evaluation for the South Bank Centre – the complex of buildings and activities that includes the Royal Festival Hall in London – involving their education department and six inner-city secondary schools. Over three years, teachers and classes of between twenty-five and thirty students – one class from each school – had access to the resources of the Centre, including the Festival and Queen Elizabeth Halls, the Gamelan room, ensembles in rehearsal and performance and, most importantly, musicians – performers and composers from many traditions. The students were aged 11 to 12 at the start of the scheme and 13 to 14 by the end. Central to the rationale of the programme was that students should work with active musicians, that their experiences should be musically genuine, 'authentic'.

The first of five linked projects began in the autumn term, 1994 and was located around the Centre's Javanese Gamelan in the Royal Festival Hall. In an initial preparatory day one or two teachers from each of the six schools were immersed in the principles and practices of gamelan. This was followed by two days of gamelan workshops for the students and the six classes were bussed from their respective schools to the South Bank Centre. This initial impetus was followed by activities during normal school music lessons where the gamelan sessions were adapted and used as a repertory of ideas with which to compose. This pattern set a precedent for the other four projects that were to follow. An initial preparatory day for teachers was spent in anticipation of the students' spending up to two days working at the Centre, and these workshops either preceded or were followed by related work in schools.

The second project had as its focus Steve Reich's composition *City Life*. This work had recently been premiered in France and Germany and the British premiere was broadcast from the South Bank Centre on 10 May 1995. During this second project, the classes from the six schools were given the opportunity to meet and talk to Steve Reich. They heard *City Life* in final rehearsal and both before and after this event they composed and performed their own music using rhythm loops, city noises and word sounds, as to some extent does Reich himself. In this they were helped in school by members of the London Sinfonietta and two composers. Performances of students' compositions took place in June 1995 before a small but appreciative audience.

During the first part of the second year, the third project focused on 'percussion and rhythm'. An objective here was that the students become more competent in rhythmic playing and aware of a range of possible percussion techniques on various instruments. There was input from five musicians who between them visited each school three times. They included an orchestral percussionist who played in the premiere of Birtwistle's *Panic* at the Last Night of the Proms, a Chilean expert in samba, an orchestral percussionist with a particular interest in contemporary music and a West African drummer. After this preparatory work the classes visited the South Bank Centre for a rehearsal and a performance. Most of the children stayed to rehearse and perform a short piece by Harrison Birtwistle at the start of a public concert which included his new and controversial work, *Panic*, and music by Edgard Varèse.

At the start of the fourth project, 'Film', students watched a film clip, analysed it and decided where the music might come. Aided in school by film composers, they were to think about the style, the period and the feeling that the film evoked, reflect this in their music, create a score or cue sheet, write music to underscore dialogue, distinguish between music and sound effects and explore dramatic characterisation in music. As a technical basis for this they improvised and composed using drones and repetitive patterns and explored timbre, texture and varied instrumentation. This work on film culminated in a session at the South Bank Centre where students rehearsed and performed their music to the film clips projected on to a large screen.

The fifth and final project culminated in mid-July 1997 in a lively Royal Festival Hall concert advertised and run along the lines of a pop concert under the heading 'Freed Up'. The groups had been previously prepared and were accompanied in performance by four professional musicians. The school project classes now had names such as 'The Vees', 'The Outlaws' and 'The Addison All Stars'. A leaflet had been produced to show the audience something of the character of the preceding projects, 'from Gamelan to Samba, and Classical to Funk'. The idea was to celebrate the three years of music-making and to 'have fun'.

The six secondary or high schools opting into the programme study represented a typical range of inner-urban London schools. Each school initially identified one 'project' class of Year 7 students (age 11+) to follow the scheme throughout the three years. A 'control' class was also identified in each school, matched as far as possible with the project classes, having the same music teacher, being the same age, in the same academic ability band and members of classes with a similar social mix. There were, then, in total between 165 and 180 students in each of the two groups, with these numbers subject to some change as students came and went over the five projects.

Evaluating such a programme over a long time span is a complex activity and neither our methodology nor our findings can have the shiny precision of a laboratory study. However, we believe that a balance of qualitative and quantitative techniques gives the research sufficient credence to inform thinking about music education in secondary schools. Our field researcher, Dorothy Lawson, took care to avoid ecological disturbance by becoming a familiar but unobtrusive observer and participant. Unstructured and semi-structured interviews with teachers, students and visiting musicians took place in all six schools and during events at the Centre. Observations and recordings were made of the compositions and performances of the students, allowing us to assess informally any influence the projects may have had on their work. We thus had a large amount of qualitative data and we are very grateful to the teachers who supplied us with information, made us welcome to their lessons and the project meetings and gave us access to interview students.

Quantitative data was also available. Student attitude inventories were completed in school within two to four weeks following the completion of each of the five projects by both the project and control groups. They answered the following questions, putting ticks on a five-point scale for each one:

How do you feel about school in general?
How do you feel about people in your class?
How do you feel when you listen to music at home with your friends?
How do you feel about music lessons in school?

This fairly elementary instrument turned out to be valid for our purposes as a robust and easy-to-use measure of attitude, especially bearing in mind that the results from this inventory were evaluated along with other, richer sources of evidence.

On the qualitative side, the comments below are a fairly typical sample of what we observed and what students had to say to us. These can be clustered under several thematic headings.

The outside venue

It was pretty obvious from the start that just getting out of school was itself a very large bonus and also that the scale and location of the South Bank Centre had some special attractions.

It's good being in the Hall. I'd never been into something like that before. I'd been to little concerts before, but that was different.

I like the Royal Festival Hall as a building – the views and the way it's designed.

Social maturity

One clearly visible outcome was the development of social awareness and responsible involvement. By the second year the teachers all felt that the project classes were becoming more socially mature. One teacher said that his class had 'gelled' more than any other of the Year 8 classes (age 12–13). Of course, this could be a result of getting out of school together. However, there is some evidence that participation in music alongside people from other schools was having a socialising effect to the extent that students worked well together and became genuinely interested in the work of others.

> I like performing in front of the other schools and listening to other people's work.

> It was great to see what other schools had done with the same film clip. They had done different things.

> The worst part was some people got the hang of it before others.

Engagement in musical processes

There were a surprising number of comments about the intrinsic musical processes and the value of these.

> I remember the Gamelan and Maleeswe. You don't often get a beat in music lessons. It was good having different languages and dancing. Ade did the drum beats. You could let yourself go.

> You can try things out and experiment with more ideas.

> What was different about this project was combining different instruments. You can make it up and it's not right or wrong.

> I liked the Gamelan best, the little instruments and the room. It's like being in an actual place. It's a different atmosphere. You take your shoes off. I always wanted to be the one playing the drum. I'd never done anything like that before in my life.

> Work in class has helped me to understand the musicians and the way they play.

> You use numbers instead of letters. That was different and we had to concentrate. Once you knew that then it flowed. Some instruments were very loud and some were soft. That music was more like a religious soft music. It was like stepping into a temple. It was very relaxing. If I had a headache then it would make me calm.

> It was easy to play and Andy showed us what to do. I liked the gong and the metallophones.

> When we did our own pieces on classroom instruments we started with note 'C' as number one. We took out notes from the metallophones and dismantled the

drum kit. We made the instruments sound similar to the Gamelan and then played in front of the school.

I thought that *City Life* would be more classical. But the piece was like normal everyday life. I remember the sirens – and he's famous for doing it!

The dances in Maleeswe were good. That was different. It was good to learn something with feet and clapping and words. Learning it was serious, but once we got it, it was fun.

The class chose a film and then we split into smaller groups and created different things. Composing the music was easier with an image to look at.

It was a 'panic' – fast and loud. It would go a bit more relaxed and then manic again.

My brother who is in primary school is going to visit the Gamelan at the Royal Festival Hall. I said 'you're going to love it, that's one of my favourites'. He said 'I don't like music'. I said 'but this is different'.

Regard for musicians

These young people were happy to give their allegiance to and admire the participating musicians, whatever the musical idiom. Many of these students were very committed to some form of pop music but this did not inhibit them from responding to contemporary western music or an African or South American drummer.

You get to know the person. They all had different ideas. It's an honour for them to come in.

Paul Clarvis was really cool. When I saw the concert I went home and told Mum about it. I said that I liked it and that I don't get to hear or see anything like that usually. Paul didn't have to dress all smart for his performance. He was good because he was out in his brightly coloured clothes and just being himself, so everyone liked him.

It was great to meet John – who did the music for Hamish Macbeth which I see on TV every Sunday. And Errollyn Wallen had played with Eternal!

Nobody thought they were above us. It was just like talking to a normal person. They were really down to earth.

We feel like composers. When you see and work with different musicians you get to behave like them a bit.

The music-making

The quality of much of the music made by these young people impressed itself upon the teachers, members of audiences and the researchers. As we might expect, there were clear relationships between the students' compositions and the project activities. For example, following the 'Gamelan' and *City Life* projects *ostinati* were much in evidence as were layered textures and speech and street sounds. Titles showed the influence of *City Life*: 'The Modern Age', 'Check out the Jungle Man', 'Street Beat'. Rhythm patterns absorbed during the percussion project became rhythmic anchors in many student compositions.

By the half-way point – eighteen months into the scheme – it was clear that many of the students were deeply involved in music-making. They played, stamped or clapped with rhythmic drive. What is more, they sang, something rarely observed amongst students in secondary schools. They sang in tune, with breath-supported vocal production, with a range of tonal shading and experiencing obvious enjoyment. There was some part singing. The musicians involved in the projects were able to signal unrehearsed as well as prepared changes during performance and students could manage quite elaborate cross rhythms. Whatever rocky moments there may have been, performances hung together. They were also critically aware. Typical comments included: 'it sounded better than last time', 'they played well together', 'the voices need to be louder', 'I liked the way it was joined together', 'it sounded really brilliantly dancy and rhythmical'.

Student attitudes

This study was not commissioned until the Gamelan project was just about underway. It was therefore not possible to have a true pre-project attitude measure as a base-line. However, it seems reasonable to infer from inspection of the data at the first point of measurement that the project and 'control' groups had similar attitudes at the outset. One initial research question was: is there a significant difference in attitudes towards school music and music outside of school over the time span of the five projects? Figure 7 shows changes in central tendency over time and the relationship between project and control classes for three of the schools from which we had really dependable data over the whole three-year period.

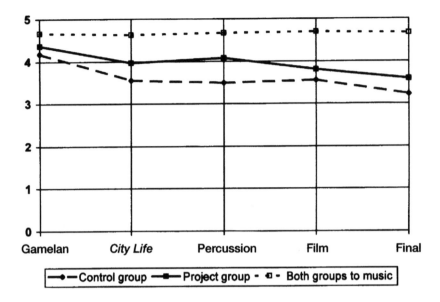

Figure 7 Attitudes of both groups to music and each group to music in school

Only the question about music lessons in school shows any significant change in central tendency over the five projects. Both control and project classes show a significant decline in attitude to music in schools between the first and final attitude measure.[1] More important than these indications of central tendency is the increase in levels of variance for the control groups. This is significantly different from the project classes for every project except the 'Gamelan' at the start of the scheme. Figure 8 shows that in their attitudes to school music the project classes tend to retain the lower levels of variance found initially in Year 7 while the matched (control) classes follow the predicted pattern of increasing variance.[2] The project classes maintain a greater degree of homogeneity: that is to say, their scores are not only generally higher than in the other groups but are less scattered across the five-point scale. This finding suggests greater agreement as to the value of 'school music'.

These quantifiable data reinforce what teachers and students were telling us in conversation. Several teachers came to believe that their project classes became more responsible and socially mature during the three years and the variance levels seem to support this view. The evidence suggests that over the first three years of secondary or high school the project classes produced fewer individuals with extreme negative attitudes to music in school. Homogeneity is an important concept here.

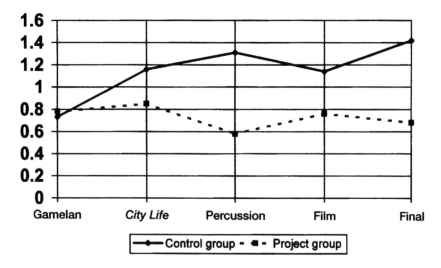

Figure 8 Levels of variance in attitudes to music in school

Students in their early teens are often difficult to manage in schools because they are – attitudinally if not literally – 'all over the place'. Our measures taken along with the attitude to music in schools suggest increased social maturity and collaboration among the project classes. Overall, then, during the three-year period we found the following.

- Project and control classes all show a decline in attitude towards music in school, though the project classes significantly less so at two of the four points of measurement.
- The project classes retained higher levels of group homogeneity in attitudes to music in school, to school, to peers and to music in general.
- Qualitative data support quantitative findings and indicate positive gains in social maturity, students' valuing of music, regard for musicians from a range of styles and practical musical outcomes.
- Negative attitudes centred mainly on aspects of organisational confusion.
- Behavioural problems increased in some schools, with the professional musicians not always able to manage the students in school settings.
- Class-sized groups were often uncomfortably large for the project activities.
- Planning schedules were sometimes disrupted, practical support from schools was increasingly uneven and it became progressively more difficult to make the special

arrangements to alter timetables or release students from school and transport them to and from the South Bank Centre.

- This whole initiative was limited or facilitated to a very great extent by widely variable conditions between individual schools.

There was significant variation in the effect on different schools and several communication problems between the two systems – school and the professional music world. There were also failures of communication. For example, five of the project schools were to attend a rehearsal of Birtwistle's controversial new work *Panic* and Varèse's *Ionisation*, both involving percussion playing and relating directly to previous work in schools. As it happened, the orchestral manager changed the order of the rehearsal so that at the crucial time they were rehearsing string and wind versions of Beethoven's *Grosse Fuge*, a change of plan that ruled out attending the rehearsal. This is but one instance of where differently managed groups – in this case the orchestra and the education department of the South Bank Centre – were not able to co-ordinate their schedules. There are certainly lessons here for future relationships between schools and arts organisations.

From so many angles though, the findings are encouraging, both for the South Bank Centre and the schools. Students, teachers and others attending the public events expressed positive views. The teachers thought there were social benefits, particularly when working with 'real' musicians in school and at the Centre. In more than one school it was felt that the status of music had been raised by involvement with the project. From interviews and observations our impression was that there were indeed attitudinal and musical gains. Many students appeared to become musically more skilled and responsive and the contact with 'real' musical worlds was thought by teachers, the project team and the evaluating observers to have enhanced both musical and social awareness for many students.

The status of contemporary 'serious' music was also raised in the minds of students. For example, in discussion with Steve Reich following the rehearsal of his *City Life*, the composer was asked how much he was paid to produce the piece. His answer left the students in no doubt that composers were real people and that composing could really be a lucrative activity, though one involving some hard work. This itself was a revelation.

The South Bank Centre venture appeared in many ways to be a catalyst, bringing endemic problems to the surface as well as opening up new experiences for students and teachers alike. The evidence suggests that the strong musical focus of the South Bank Centre programme may have helped to overcome the difficulty of managing adolescent groups, although frequently taking students out of school and having prestigious visitors engaging in classroom work may be alternative or at least complementary explanations.

Many of the teachers thought their own musical development was enhanced, that the programme had raised their musical 'game' along with that of the students. As one said: 'It is difficult to express in just a few words the huge impact this has had on my pupils and myself. To experience such a varied programme of events over a long period has enriched my own musicianship and will enhance all my teaching in the future.'

The issue of authenticity

The comment above is indicative of a widespread need. Secondary school music teachers may find themselves uncomfortably veering between their own musical specialism (which may or may not be valued by students) and an insecure 'generalism', for instance, in popular music and what has come to be known as 'world musics'. Although Hargreaves applies a 'specialist-generalist' continuum (Hargreaves 1996) to primary schools, we could equally see this in the secondary school, where music teachers are inevitably specialists in one or two kinds of music but also generalists in the much wider range of music required both by the curriculum and by our culturally diverse society. We might speculate that this lack of musical 'authenticity' accounts in part for the tendency for secondary students to become progressively disenchanted with music in school.

Genuine musical experience has within it something of metaphorical richness. Without this quality of experience music education is impoverished. Indeed, there is a long history of negative attitudes to school music on the part of pupils, especially in secondary schools (Schools Council 1968; Francis 1987; Ross 1995). In a report of a recent study of the arts in five secondary schools, Ross and Kamba assert that for music 'the enjoyment factor remains unchanged and disappointingly low' (Ross and Kamba 1997). We did not find this negative picture among the students in our evaluation of the South Bank Centre programme. Even among those students who were not part of the scheme, attitudes were fairly positive (see Figure 7).

Even so, whether primary, secondary or tertiary, very few schools and colleges can now be musical islands. We might consider how to invest resources differently, for example, involving musicians, individuals and communities as part of a music education network, rather than seeing them as exceptional novelties. Colleges and secondary schools in particular might become facilitating agencies rather than sole 'providers'.

Music teaching in inner-city secondary schools is challenging, complex and taxing, whilst there is a richness of resources beyond the school gates if we know how to find and utilise it. The students we studied had access to specialist professional music expertise and to a range of styles which it would not be possible to replicate authentically in every or indeed any school, certainly not on the costly scale of this programme. It so happens that the South Bank Centre programme involved professional musicians. But there are many musicians in communities who could also contribute to the authenticity of music in schools. Most communities have rich seams of music-making ready to be mined. The resources of nearby schools might also be pooled, especially the musical expertise of teachers.

Music is not a single entity easily reduced to work in conventional classrooms but a multiplicity of activities, each requiring some specialist know-how, varying group size and different levels and types of equipment. How can one teacher and every single school provide access to such musical diversity as, for example, gamelan, steel pans, standard western orchestral instruments in all their variety, a range of choral experience, small groups playing rock and pop and possibly jazz, Indian music and the musics of Africa and the Pacific? Very rarely can students be said to be having a musically authentic experience. No wonder 'school music' appears to many young people as a sub-culture separated from music out there in the world, abstracted by the constraints of classroom and curriculum and subject to very curious arrangements for assessment. We have to do better than this. We should consider involving musicians of various kinds as part of a music education *network*, rather than see them as exotic novelties.

To draw on resources of this kind would require agencies outside of schools to take account of the restrictions of school organisation and to plan carefully and well in advance. It would also be necessary to look critically at the structure and function of schools themselves. If we can achieve this there may be considerable potential for future collaboration between educational and musical agencies. However, the tension between school music and other music is currently amplified structurally within the educational system.

> Represented here are two distinct approaches to curriculum innovation which appear to be in tension – the one a nationally engineered, standardised approach to a curriculum devised in non-school settings and imposed with the force of law; the other a locally diverse basket of activities devised in collaborations between professional musicians in school and joined on a voluntaristic basis.
>
> (Kushner 1994: 45)

Saville Kushner sees these collaborative activities as educationally rich, permitting children to engage with music in their own way and at their own speed. There may be little if any curriculum sequencing towards pre-specified learning outcomes. Such projects tend to be broadly process-based rather than geared to narrowly defined and standardised 'products'. Complex music may be 'deconstructed' – for example, involvement over time with an opera production can have different levels of meaning for different individuals. Such musical activities are not only more open-ended but they may also be perceived as 'authentic', involving 'real' instruments, 'real' music, 'real' musicians and 'real' music-making settings, unlike the cumulative and incremental teaching that characterises an institutional curriculum. Although I would link authenticity with the quality of musical experience, there is a sense in which quality depends on a depth of musical understanding which is only likely among insiders to a particular way of 'musicing'.

Institutional treadmills

Our experience with the South Bank Centre project and our knowledge of similar ventures is in sharp contrast with formal, institutionalised music education. From a disturbing number of sources flows criticism of music teaching. For example, in British secondary schools music is perceived as uneven, with wide variation in curriculum content and prone to low educational expectations. Inspectors have raised questions about the quality of work, the conditions under which music is taught and the morale of secondary music teachers (Mills 1994). Among several negative observations of the quality of music teaching in secondary school are teachers underestimating pupils' abilities, with too much time spent on non-musical activities and poor performance of badly chosen material (OFSTED 1992–3). Reports of government inspectors sustain these criticisms. 'The curriculum in Year 7 was often less challenging than that in primary schools, and its demand increased insufficiently in Years 8 and 9' (OFSTED 1995). In 1996 achievement was still thought to be too low and 'pupils' understanding of musical concepts, shown through composition, talk and performance, does not develop beyond that expected in Year 5 and Year 6' (OFSTED 1996). By 1997 we are told that standards 'remain poor in too many schools at Key Stage 3' (OFSTED 1997).

Our impressions from a teacher training perspective coincide with these more 'official' findings. The supervision each year at the University of London Institute of Education of up to forty music graduates intending to become secondary or high school music teachers leads us to believe that music education in these schools is

indeed very patchy. Of course, there are bright exceptions, outstanding teachers often –
though not always – working in conducive settings. But it seems unwise to predicate
the standards of any profession on the performance of the extraordinary person.
Surely in any other job we would expect an effective contribution by the majority of
those engaged in it, not only by a few bright stars. We are also impressed by the
musicality, the positive attitudes of our students each year, their development as teachers during the course and their enthusiastic and energetic approach to teaching music.
And we are conscious of the alarming difference in the same people two or three years
later, when the shine has rubbed off and the system has ground their energy away.

We need to look realistically at what is possible. In most British state secondary
schools a teacher has five to seven classes of around thirty children each day, perhaps
upward of 600 different pupils every week. The same can be said of most American
elementary schools. This teacher is expected to be a versatile musician, able to work in
the music of a number of cultures and at the same time to be a systematic educator
making sure that each individual is engaged in an integrated music curriculum at a
challenging level. In addition to this 'normal' teaching commitment and the regular
pastoral and organisational duties of a school teacher, there is the management of
instrumental teaching schemes running on a parallel timetable, leading several extra-
curricular groups and the production of musical events throughout the year. These
activities are usually planned and prepared in out-of-timetable time and are rarely
offset against the normal teaching load. Of course, teachers of, say, mathematics will
say that they also have to mark work. But marking paper work is not the same drain-
ing and demanding activity that face-to-face coaching entails, as music teachers strive
to meet deadlines for end of term concerts, shows and other public events. Doing both
jobs of music teacher and director of music rolled into one is onerous, especially when
people are only paid for one of them.

In American schools the situation tends to be very different. Here the system tends
to separate out the main musical activities of composing, performing and audience-
listening, usually concentrating on performance. The result is that students tend to get
a limited view of what music is and how it functions. In the United States middle and
high school music is mostly an 'elective', usually a choice between band or choir and
sometimes 'general music'. Once the activity is chosen students can expect up to four
time-tabled rehearsals a week, usually in rooms designed for the purpose.

I would resist this arrangement as a model for several reasons, principally because
the sole activity is usually rehearsal of a limited repertoire towards a distant performance date, whereas in the UK we now have a tradition that extols the value of
composing, audience-listening *and* performing. Divorcing one musical activity from

another seems an odd way to engage in a single multi-faceted endeavour, that of music education. There appears to be relatively little interest among United States researchers in evaluating the attitudes of students to their music programmes and a major publication on research in music education makes no substantial reference to this issue (Colwell 1992). Rather more effort seems to go into public justification of these programmes and in trying to explain and improve enrolment patterns. Research now in progress in my own department suggests that many American school students experience boredom in music electives, often through sheer satiation brought about by repetition in endless rehearsal of the same few pieces. Even so, they may still be happy to opt for music, sometimes because they can more easily get higher grades, or perhaps because there is no written work, or because they sometimes get out of school on band or choir excursions.

There have, of course, been many missed opportunities. In Britain there were once widespread instrumental teaching services organised by Local Education Authorities. This work could have extended to teaching groups which would not only study instrumental technique but would rehearse and perform, compose and listen to the music of other people. This possibility was largely disregarded and with rare exceptions, such as the experimental Tower Hamlets string teaching project in London's East End (Swanwick and Jarvis 1990), instrumental teachers were not integrated into the fabric of school curriculums and timetables. Instead they functioned much as they do in today's more privatised system, operating on the edge of the educational 'mainstream' yet important for the image of a school. In the United States there have been several projects and publications designed to broaden and integrate curriculum activities. The effect of these appears, however, to have been minimal, except in some junior high schools and schools for younger children. Even there, teaching methodologies seem to shape the curriculum in different ways and there are often competing claims for the musical high ground by followers of Orff, Kodály and Dalcroze, or the users of schemes published by Silver Burdett, Macmillan, and so on.

In spite of all these programmes, and no matter what teaching scheme is used, teachers are still left with a fundamental choice as to whether or not they regard their job as getting people going in musical discourse. If not, then they are teaching something else. If so, then having sound principles matters more than any particular method. The principles *are* important. This is brought home to us forcefully when they are absent from an educational transaction.

The witty picture by Sempé (Figure 9) says a great deal about certain types of traditional music teaching. It is by no means true only for instrumental instruction. The insignificant student is coached by the musical guru who is the mediator between her

Figure 9 The music lesson: *Wladimir Hernsingern and Brigitte* by Sempé

and the great composer. It is going to take many years for the little girl to be fully initiated. We do not know whether the first principle – care for music – is in place or not. This all depends on how the teacher plays and how the student is helped to play. There is certainly not much evidence here of either the second or third principles in action. Neither student autonomy nor musical fluency is likely to be at a premium in this kind of lesson. Nor is there likely to be a range of activities such as might constitute a comprehensive musical education. I doubt that this particular student is going to listen in audience to music or discuss it with her teacher and she is very unlikely to be asked to improvise or compose. She may well give up playing within a few years. Yet it does not always have to be thus.

We know better songs than these

A line like this occurs in the film *Educating Rita*. We do often suspect that things could be better, might be different, would be marvellous . . . if only! But even in less than perfect conditions it is an enormous advantage to know what we are looking for, to understand what sort of activity music is and what principled teaching feels like. I have attempted to get this as clear as I can. This is how the thesis looks when stripped down to essentials:

- Music is a form of symbolic discourse.
- At its heart is the process of metaphor which occurs in three ways: tones are transformed into 'tunes', or gestures; gestures evolve into new structures; these structures can give rise to significant experiences as they relate to our personal and cultural histories.
- The three metaphorical transformations are audible though the layers of observable musical elements to which they give rise: materials, expression, form and value.
- Music arises in a social context; however, because of its metaphorical nature music is not merely culturally reflective but can be creatively interpreted and produced.
- It follows that there are three essential principles for music educators: care for music as discourse, care for the musical discourse of students, care for musical fluency.
- An education committed to the quality of musical experience is mindful that students move between all four layers of musical discourse.
- Configured as an assessment model, these layers give validity when evaluating the work of students and in self-evaluation.

- Research based on this theory of musical mind supports the idea of an integrated music curriculum where students compose, perform and respond to music as audience-listeners.
- The contemporary plurality of 'musics' requires a redefinition of the relationship between music-making in the community and formal music education in the studio and classroom.

Yes, there is still a role for teachers! (See Figure 10.) They can help people get further inside musical discourse than they otherwise might if unaided. There is a real job to do in studio and classroom and out there among those who make and disseminate music. In the private music school in Brazil which I discussed in the previous chapter, all the pupils performed and composed and they all listened to, analysed and discussed music in their 'musicalisation' classes. The school was lively with all kinds of music, not a musical sub-culture but a musical *super-culture*. The place hummed with musical discourse. And the students and the parents knew this and valued it. Private music teaching does not have to be a string of individuals passing through, as if visiting the dentist.

As far as school and college classrooms are concerned, the contemporary issue of musical plurality is crucial. While recognising the social roots of all music we may sometimes have to cut off cultural labels and help shift out of the way some of the

Figure 10 The autodidact: *André* by Sempé

barriers of tribal possessiveness and exclusiveness. One strategy is to recognise that, in spite of the apparent diversity of much of the world's music, we can still identify elements which, though they may appear in quite different contexts, are common to much music. We can think of repeated melodic or rhythmic patterns, the use of scales or modes, of chorus or antiphonal effects, call and response, dance rhythms, drones, effective changes of texture or timbre. We can extend our idea of what Orff called limited structures, to take in ragas, whole tone scales, note-rows, jazz and blues chord sequences and so on. In these ways we can extend our expressive range and in so doing come to have a better understanding of the minds of other people by entering into their musical procedures. The history and cultural context of music can only be approached through the doors and windows of particular performances.

In organisational terms we have to consider how best to use the resources we have and be clear about extra resources we need to find. The ideal would be for every school to give or facilitate access to a range of authentic and viable instrumental and vocal groupings led by confident teachers. Students would elect into at least one of these activities. With the exception of some choral work these will not be large groups but will often be small enough to be managed as practical instrumental workshops, probably between eight and fifteen students. Within the focus of these quite specific activities they will perform, compose and listen to and discuss music from many sources. Some of these activities will be on school premises, though by no means all. This sharing of available resources in the community would be of great value to primary school teachers who often feel uncertain about their general musical competence and to so-called specialist teachers who feel de-skilled by the growing list of 'world musics' in which it may wrongly be assumed that they are 'expert'.

We also need to exploit the possibilities of information technology. We can see its contribution in two broad areas. One is the extension of individualised learning which resonates with the second principle – that of student autonomy. The second contribution of information technology is the extension of instrumental resources in a radical way, giving us instant accompaniments, quite new tonal effects and undreamed of combinations of sounds, the use of computers to assist in the processes of musical composition and performance. And this can be achieved without going through the high-wire act of bringing it all off in real time.

How does the technology stand the test of our three principles? The first of our principles, care for music, is at hazard only if we forget that micro-technology is a tool and not an end in itself. It is very easy to progressively mechanise human imagination out of existence and to use pre-recorded loops and patterns which, whilst they may serve the purposes of a certain kind of instant music-making, certainly do not develop expressive range or structural sensitivity. But the computer can also be used both to stimulate compositional processes and to facilitate editing and notating. It can also translate visual metaphors of music into sound.

This is all very different from using the computer only to have students grind away at notationally driven composition – a form of sequenced instruction that the computer does all too well. This flies in the face of the principle of fluency and also of the first principle, care for music as discourse. To be able to say in music only what we can write in notation negates both musical expressiveness and the musical discourse of students. We should be looking for technological progress to release teachers and students from drudgery, not increasing it. People might then be more free to produce and respond to lively music which can play its part in promoting eventfulness and conviviality while at the same time enhancing sensibility and extending the mind.

There will be resistance to change, not least because our institutions are locked into fairly rigid systems. One effect of the drift towards centralised school curricula – though presumably not intended – is that teaching tends to take place almost entirely in school classrooms. Certainly teacher trainees in the UK and elsewhere are constrained to spend most of their time 'on school premises' and that is where teachers are inspected and expected to be at work. Furthermore, since every school is now a small business run in competition with those nearby, it seems unlikely that sharing of teaching expertise and other resources will be easy. Why should one school enhance the profile of another? Yet there is a musical richness beyond individual school gates if only we could more systematically find and utilise it. This could be achieved within the requirements of National Standards or a National Curriculum. What has to evolve is the greater co-ordination of resources in and out of school and a new attitude to how we use people and time.

Perhaps enlightened educational and political mandarins from various countries could get together groups of competent and experienced people to look at alternative timetable models and ways in which access to the arts, including music in all its diversity, might more profitably be organised in the curriculum and the community. Music is not the only activity where the division between curricula and the extra-curricular could helpfully start to be eroded. The conventional wisdom of how things should be is ripe for examination.

However, no shuffling of time and resources can replace the integrity of the teacher and the quality of the educational transaction, whether in studio, school, college or community. For ultimately, teaching music *musically* can only be done by those who care for and understand that the human activity we call music is a rich form of discourse.

I hope the 'essential philosophy' mapped out in this book will help and inform, not only those who teach, but also those who facilitate and support teaching, including institutional managers, local communities, arts agencies and parents. For the future of the human species depends on the capacity of its members to make metaphorical transformations, to ask the question 'what if?', to go beyond cultural replication towards cultural renewal. Music has its part to play in this discourse, in these 'conversations' which define what it is to be human.

Notes

1 A Wilcoxon Matched-Pairs Signed-Ranks Test for both groups gives $p < 0.001$. This compares strikingly with unchanging high positive attitudes to 'music at home with your friends'. There are statistically significant differences between the scores of the control and project groups for the '*City Life*' and 'Percussion' projects. (A Mann–Whitney U Test gives $p < 0.03$ for '*City Life*' and $p < 0.001$ for 'Percussion'.)

2 A Levine Test for the significance of difference in variance confirmed significantly greater homogeneity of attitude among project students, with 'Percussion' at $p < 0.001$, 'Film' at $p < 0.01$ and the 'Final' project at $p < 0.03$.

References

Abbs, P. (1994) *The Educational Imperative*, London: Falmer Press.

ACAC (1996) *Exemplification of Standards in Music: Key Stage 3*, Cardiff: Welsh School Curriculum and Asssessment Authority.

ACAC (1997) *Optional Tests and Tasks in Music: Key Stage 3*, Cardiff: Welsh Curriculum and Assessment Authority.

Best, D. (1989) 'Feeling and reason in the arts: the rationality of feeling', in P. Abbs (ed.), *The Symbolic Order*, London: Falmer Press.

Blacking, J. (1995) 'Music, culture and experience', in R. Byron (ed.) *Selected Papers of John Blacking*, Chicago and London: University of Chicago Press.

Blumer, H. (1969) *Symbolic Interactionism: Perspective and Method*, Berkeley: University of California Press.

Bowman, W. D. (1998) *Philosophical Perspectives on Music*, New York and Oxford: Oxford University Press.

Campbell, Patricia Shehan (1998) *Songs in Their Heads: Music and Its Meaning in Children's Lives*, New York and Oxford: Oxford University Press.

Capra, F. (1996) *The Web of Life*, London: HarperCollins.

Cassirer, E. (1955) *The Philosophy of Symbolic Forms* (Ralph Manheim, trans.), New Haven and London: Yale University Press.

Cavafy, C. P. (1981) 'Longings', in E. Keeley and E. Sherrard (eds), *A Greek Quintet*, Limni, Evia, Greece: Denise Harvey & Co.

Chernoff, J. M. (1979) *African Rhythm and African Sensibility*, Chicago and London: University of Chicago Press.

Colwell, R. (1992) *Handbook of Research on Music Teaching and Learning*, New York: Schirmer Books.

Cooke, D. (1959) *The Language of Music*, Oxford: Oxford University Press.

Csikszentmihalya, M. and Robinson, R. E. (1990) *The Art of Seeing*, Malibu, California: Getty.

Dewey, J. (1934) Art as Experience (1958 edn), New York: Capricorn Books.

Elliott, D. J. (1995) *Music Matters: A New Philosophy of Music Education*, New York and Oxford: Oxford University Press.

Elliott, D. J. (1997) 'Continuing matters: myths, realities, rejoinders', *Bulletin of the Council for Research in Music Education* 132: 1–37.

Empson, W. (1947) *Seven Types of Ambiguity*, London: Chatto & Windus.

Federation of Music Services and National Association of Music Educators (1998) *A Common Approach: A Framework for an Instrumental/Vocal Curriculum*, London: Faber Music Ltd.

Ferguson, D. N. (1960) *Music as Metaphor: The Elements of Expression*, Westport, Con: Greenwood Press.

Finnegan, R. (1989) *The Hidden Musicians: Music-making in an English Town*, Cambridge: Cambridge University Press.

Francis, L. J. (1987) 'The decline in attitudes towards religious education among 8–15 year olds', *Educational Studies* 13, 2.

Gans, H. J. (1974) *High Culture and Popular Culture*, New York: Basic Books.

Gardner, H. (1993) *The Unschooled Mind* (first published 1991), London: Fontana.

Godwin, J. (1986) *Music, Mysticism and Magic: A Sourcebook*, London: Routledge.

Goodman, N. (1976) *Languages of Art: An Approach to a Theory of Symbols*, Indianapolis, IN: Hackett Publishing.

Grahame, K. (1973, first published 1895) *The Golden Age*, London: Bodley Head.

Green, L. (1997) *Music, Gender, Education*, Cambridge: Cambridge University Press.

Hargreaves, D. J. (1996) 'The development of artistic and musical competence', in I. deLiege and J. A. Sloboda (eds), *Musical Beginnings: The Origins and Development of Musical Competence*, Oxford: Oxford University Press.

Hentschke, L. (1993) *Musical Development: Testing a Model in the Audience-listening Setting*, Unpublished PhD, University of London, Institute of Education.

Housman, A. E. (1992/ 1965) 'Eight O' Clock', in *The Collected Poems of A.E. Housman*, New York, Chicago and San Francisco: Holt, Rinehart & Winston Inc.

Jacques-Dalcroze, E. (1915) *Rhythm, Music and Education*, (H. F. Rubinstein, trans.) (1967 edn), London: Riverside Press.

Kirchhoff, C. (1988) 'The school and college band: wind band pedagogy in the United States', in J. T. Gates (ed.), *Music Education in the United States: Contemporary Issues*, Tuscaloosa: University of Alabama Press.

Koestler, A. (1964) *The Act of Creation*, New York: Macmillan.

Kress, G. (1985) *Linguistic Processes in Sociocultural Practice*, Oxford: Oxford University Press.

Kress, G. and Van Leeuwen, T. (1996) *Reading Images: The Grammar of Visual Design*, London and New York: Routledge.

Kushner, S. (1994) 'Against better judgement: how a centrally prescribed music curriculum works against teacher development', *International Journal of Music Education* 23: 34–45.

Kwami, R. M. (1989) *African Music, Education and the School Curriculum*, Unpublished PhD, University of London, Institute of Education.

Langer, S. K. (1942) *Philosophy in a New Key*, New York and Cambridge, MA: Mentor Books and Harvard University Press.

Langer, S. K. (1967) *Mind: An Essay on Human Feeling* (Vol. 1), Baltimore: Johns Hopkins Press.

Leonhard, C. and House, R. W. (1959) *Foundations and Principles of Music Education*, New York: McGraw-Hill.

Loane, B. (1982) 'The absurdity of rank order assessment', in J. Paynter (ed.), *Music in the Secondary School Curriculum*, Cambridge: Cambridge University Press.

Mac Cormac, E. R. (*c*1985) *A Cognitive Theory of Metaphor*, Cambridge, Mass: A Bradford Book.

Martin, P. J. (1995) *Sounds and Society*, Manchester: Manchester University Press.

McAuley, J. (1965) 'New Guinea', in D. Stewart (ed.), *Poetry in Australia, Vol 2, Modern Australian Verse*, Berkeley and Los Angeles: University of California Press.

McLaughlin, T. (1970) *Music and Communication*, London: Faber.

Mead, M. (1942) 'Our educational emphases in primitive perspective', *American Journal of Sociology* 48: 633–9.

MENC (1994) *National Standards for Arts Education*, Reston, VA, USA: Music Educators National Conference.

Merriam, A. P. (1964) *The Anthropology of Music*, Chicago: Northwestern University Press.

Meyer, L. B. (1956) *Emotion and Meaning in Music* (1973 edn), Chicago and London: University of Chicago and University of California Press.

Mills, J. (1991) *Music in the Primary School*, Cambridge: Cambridge University Press.

Mills, J. (1994) 'Music in the National Curriculum: the first year', *British Journal of Music Education* 11, 3: 191–6.

Nattiez, J.-J. (1987/1990) *Music and Discourse: Towards a Semiology of Music* (Carolyn Abbate, trans.), Princeton: Princeton University Press.

Oakeshot, M. (1992) *Rationalism in Politics and Other Essays*, London: Methuen.

OFSTED (1992–3) *Music – Key Stages 1, 2 and 3*, London: HMSO.

OFSTED (1995) *The Annual Report of Her Majesty's Chief Inspector of Schools, 1993/94*, London: HMSO.

OFSTED (1996) *The Annual Report of Her Majesty's Chief Inspector of Schools, 1994/5*, London: HMSO.

OFSTED (1997) *The Annual Report of Her Majesty's Chief Inspector of Schools, 1995/6*, London: HMSO.

Ortony, A. (ed.) (1979) *Metaphor and Thought*, Cambridge: Cambridge University Press.

Papapanayiotou, X. (1998) *The Acquisition of Musical Preferences: A Study of Three Age Groups in the Social and Cultural Environment of Greece*, Unpublished PhD, University of London, Institute of Education.

Passmore, J. (1991) *Serious Art: A Study of the Concept in All the Major Arts*, London: Duckworth.

Paynter, J. (1997) 'The form of finality: a context for music education', *British Journal of Music Education* 14, 1: 5–21.

Piaget, J. (1951) *Play, Dreams and Imitation in Childhood* (Norton Library, 1962 edn), New York: Norton & Co.

Plummeridge, C. (1991) *Music Education in Theory and Practice*, London: Falmer Press.

Polanyi, M. and Prosch, H. (1975) *Meaning*, Chicago: University of Chicago Press.

Popper, K. (1972) *Objective Knowledge*, Oxford: Clarendon Press.

Pratt, G. (1990) *Aural Awareness: Principles and Practice*, Milton Keynes: Open University Press.

Priest, P. (1989) 'Playing by ear: Its nature and application to instrumental learning', *British Journal of Music Education* 6, 2: 173–91.

Reid, L. A. (1986) *Ways of Understanding and Education*, University of London Institute of Education: Heinemann.

Reimer, B. (1989) *A Philosophy of Music Education* (1989 edn), Englewood Cliffs, N.J.: Prentice Hall.

Ross, M. (1984) *The Aesthetic Impulse*, Oxford: Pergamon.

Ross, M. (1995) 'What's wrong with school music?', *British Journal of Music Education* 12, 3: 185–201.

Ross, M. and Kamba, M. (1997) *State of the Arts in Five English Secondary Schools*, Exeter: University of Exeter.

Sacks, S. (ed.) (1979) *On Metaphor*, Chicago and London: University of Chicago Press.

Said, E. W. (1993) *Culture and Imperialism*, London: Chatto & Windus.

SCAA (1996a) *Exemplification of Standards in Music: Key Stage 3*, London: School Curriculum and Asssessment Authority.

SCAA (1996b) *Optional Tests and Tasks in Music: Key Stage 3*, London: School Curriculum and Assessment Authority.

Schools Council (1968) *Enquiry One: The Young Schoolleavers*, London: HMSO.

Scruton, R. (1997) *The Aesthetics of Music*, Oxford: Clarendon Press.

Silva, C. Cavalieri França (1998) *Composing, Performing and Audience-listening as Symmetrical Indicators of Musical Understanding*, Unpublished PhD University of London, Institute of Education.

Stavrides, M. (1995) *The Interaction of Audience-listening and Composing: A Study in Cyprus Schools*, Unpublished PhD, University of London, Institute of Education.

Storr, A. (1976) *The Dynamics of Creation*, Harmondsworth: Penguin.

Storr, A. (1992) *Music and the Mind*, London: HarperCollins.

Swanwick, K. (1979) *A Basis for Music Education*, London: Routledge.

Swanwick, K. (1983) *The Arts in Education: Dreaming or Wide Awake?*, London: University of London, Institute of Education.

Swanwick, K. (1988) *Music, Mind and Education*, London: Routledge.

Swanwick, K. (1994) *Musical Knowledge: Intuition, Analysis and Music Education*, London and New York: Routledge.

Swanwick, K. (1997) 'Assessing musical quality in the National Curriculum', *British Journal of Music Education* 14, 3.

Swanwick, K. and Jarvis, C. (1990) *The Tower Hamlets String Teaching Project: A Research Report*, London: University of London Institute of Education.

Swanwick, K. and Tillman, J. (1986) 'The sequence of musical development: a study of children's composition', *British Journal of Music Education* 3, 3: 305–39.

Thompson, K. (1984) 'An analysis of group instrumental teaching', *British Journal of Music Education* 1, 2: 153–71.

Walker, R. (1996) 'Music education freed from colonialism: a new praxis', *International Journal of Music Education* 27: 2–15.

Walker, R. (1998) 'Swanwick puts music education back in its western prison – a reply', *International Journal of Music Education* 31: 59–65.

Index